PROMISES TO KEEP

PROMISES TO KEEP

SAVING SOCIAL SECURITY'S DREAM

*by Marshall N. Carter
and William G. Shipman*

REGNERY PUBLISHING, INC.
Washington, D.C.

Copyright © 1996 by State Street Boston Corporation

Library of Congress Cataloging-in-Publication Data
Carter, Marshall N., 1940–
    Promises to keep : saving social security's dream / Marshall N.
Carter and William G. Shipman.
        p.   cm.
    ISBN 0-89526-438-2
    1. Old age pensions—United States.   2. Pensions—United States.
3. Social security—United States.   I. Shipman, William G., 1945–
    . II. Title.
HD7105.35.U6C36   1996
368.4'3'00973—dc20   96-32343
                                                                        CIP

Published in the United States by
Regnery Publishing, Inc.
An Eagle Publishing Company
422 First Street, SE, Suite 300
Washington, DC 20003

Distributed to the trade by
National Book Network
4720-A Boston Way
Lanham, MD 20706

Printed on acid-free paper.
Manufactured in the United States of America

10 9 8 7 6 5 4 3 2 1

Books are available in quantity for promotional or premium use. Write to
Director of Special Sales, Regnery Publishing, Inc., 422 First Street, SE, Suite
300, Washington, DC 20003, for information on discounts and terms or call
(202) 546-5005.

This book is dedicated to my two children, Christina and Marshall, and their generation's hope for a bright retirement future.
—MARSHALL N. CARTER

This book is dedicated to my son, Hammer, and his 1996 graduating class of Saint Mark's School.
—WILLIAM G. SHIPMAN

CONTENTS

PART II

PREFACE

A T STATE STREET Bank and Trust Co., we have been working to provide secure retirement incomes for Americans since 1792. For more than two centuries, investing for retirement has been a crucial part of our business.

As the largest custodian of pension funds in the United States, and as a custodian of pension funds in seventy-one countries throughout the world, we at State Street understand the financial, political, and demographic issues that are simultaneously exerting pressure on retirement systems around the globe. Our firm, State Street Global Advisors (SSGA), which manages over $270 billion, is constantly involved in the discussion, economics, and finance of achieving the necessary level of wealth for a dignified retirement.

This book is a natural outgrowth of our work on retirement issues. Our goal is to shed light on this difficult and challenging topic. We write it in an effort to help educate people everywhere. We believe that America and other countries throughout the world will benefit greatly from an open and honest debate about how best to deal with the problem of providing all citizens with a secure retirement.

While considering possible solutions to our retirement problem, we have been guided by three principles that we believe are valued by a civil society:

- ❖ The first principle is that the elderly are able to retire with financial security.
- ❖ The second principle is that younger workers should be able to keep the fruits of their labor.
- ❖ The third principle is that the economy should not be unreasonably or unnecessarily burdened by achieving the first two principles.

In our view, any and all suggestions to solve Social Security's problems should be considered if they meet these principles.

This book has been a collaborative effort of many talented people at State Street and elsewhere. One of our most productive discussions was in the summer of 1995 when we convened some of the country's finest minds on this topic. Coming together at State Street for an intense brainstorming session were Peter Ferrara, general counsel and chief economist at Americans for Tax Reform; John Goodman, president of the National Center for Policy Analysis; Dorcas Hardy, former commissioner of Social Security; and Bruce Schobel, former Social Security actuary. Much of what took place in that room is in this book.

We are grateful to Dallas Salisbury, president of the Employee Benefits Research Institute and chair of the American Savings Education Council; Julie Domenick, senior vice-president for legislative affairs at the Investment Company Institute; and Richard Parker, senior fellow and lecturer at the John F. Kennedy School of Government at Harvard.

We also owe a debt of gratitude to many of our friends and colleagues at State Street who helped in the creation of this work, including David A. Spina, president and chief operating officer; James J. Darr, executive vice-president; and John Towers, chief counsel. All offered excellent advice. F. Gregory Ahern, senior vice-president for Industry Affairs and Marketing Services, ably coordinated the project. Nick Lopardo, chairman of State Street Global Advisors, was a visionary throughout. His commitment to finding a solution to the Social Security problem inspired many of our efforts.

Also at State Street, we received support from Lenny Glynn, Beth Reynolds, Dan Miller, and Ann Mastrovich—an ardent supporter from the beginning.

We are indebted to Neal Freeman and Bill Dunn for assisting with the initial draft of the book.

And we are grateful to Charlie Kenney, who worked with us to edit and revise the book. Charlie kept us focused on delivering our message, challenged our positions, and made us defend them before they became part of this book. He was able and untiring in his efforts.

Bruce Schobel's efforts also deserve special attention. Bruce's knowledge and professionalism are extraordinary, and he was always there to answer the peculiar question and thoroughly research the difficult problem.

The proceeds of this book will go the the State Street Foundation, which supports neighborhood revitalization, education and job training and development, and youth programs in Greater Boston.

This book presents our assessment of what is wrong with Social Security, what to do about it, how, and why. This is not a doomsday book nor is it a jargon-filled, theoretical text. Rather, it is a book of hope for the future, with a specific and understandable action plan for solving the Social Security crisis once and for all. It is about freedom, empowerment, and retiring with dignity. What we propose will benefit younger workers, older retirees, their families, their communities, and their nations.

The book consists of seventeen chapters, organized into two parts. Part I deals with the origins and the workings of Social Security in the United States and throughout the world; the workers that fuel the systems; the retirees that derive benefits; and the unstoppable, unforgiving glacial force of demographics that ultimately will destroy Social Security as it now exists. In Part II we detail our action plan and present evidence that shows its implementation will work.

Let this book serve as the platform for, and an argument in, the vigorous and most necessary debate on Social Security.

Marshall N. Carter and William G. Shipman
Boston, July 1996

PROMISES TO KEEP

PART I

CHAPTER ONE

ACCEPTING THE CHALLENGE

A MERICA AND OTHER countries in the world face a financial crisis that, unchecked, ultimately will cripple national economies, public and private institutions, local communities, families, and individuals. No one will be spared.

America's Social Security system and similar programs in other countries are in serious trouble. These systems, while originally well intentioned, are irredeemably flawed in design. They are underfunded, face increasing demands from aging populations, and are headed for insolvency in the first quarter of the twenty-first century.

Consider the recent comments of the public trustees of the U.S. Social Security system in their summary of the 1995 annual report:

> During the past five years there has been a trend of deterioration in the long range financial condition of

5

> the Social Security and Medicare programs and an
> acceleration in the projected dates of exhaustion in
> the related trust funds . . . These adverse trends can
> be expected to continue and indicate the possibility of
> a future retirement crisis as the U.S. population
> begins to age rapidly. We urge that concerted action
> be taken promptly to address the critical public policy
> issues raised by the financing projections for these
> programs.

Social Security is one leg of a three-legged retirement stool, the other legs being personal savings and employer pensions. Unfortunately, the other legs are not nearly as strong as they need to be for the future, especially in the United States. The U.S. savings rate is far below that of other industrial nations, and many companies have no pension plans at all. Without repair the whole stool could collapse.

Though intended as a floor of protection on which other programs were to be built, Social Security has become the primary source of retirement income for many people. Sixty-three percent of those retired on Social Security rely on its benefits for half or more of their income. One in four depends on Social Security for 90 percent or more of his or her income.[1] One in three retirees has a pension from work.[2] While two out of three do derive income from assets and other savings,[3] the median cash value is less than $3,000.[4]

The average Social Security benefit in 1996 is only $720 a month—$8,640 a year.[5] Moreover, the true value of Social Security is declining. Relative to their taxes paid, today's retirees will get back less than their parents and grandparents did. And benefits to future retirees will be lower still, far lower than the federal government will admit today.

For decades, government and business leaders have preferred to ignore or downplay the growing problem—out of ignorance or fear or wishing it would somehow go away. It won't. The impending crisis resulting from Social Security's flawed design is inevitable.

Social Security is a pay-as-you-go system. The taxes paid by current workers are not put into accounts for their own retirement. Rather, they are spent on benefits for current retirees. Any surplus goes to other government programs. A pay-as-you-go system requires many workers per retiree to ensure low taxes as well as high benefits. As recently as 1950, there were sixteen workers for each person drawing Social Security benefits. Today, there are only three workers for each beneficiary. By 2030 there will be only two workers for each beneficiary.[6] This is the result of dropping birth rates and a steady rise in life expectancy.

Those who have attempted fixes—both Democrats and Republicans—have only covered up what's wrong. They have not cured it. President Carter said his 1977 tax hike would make Social Security "sound" for another five decades.[7] He was off by forty-four years. President Reagan assured us that his 1983 round of tax increases and other reforms would protect "the financial integrity of Social Security."[8] He was wrong, too.

Americans of all ages are beginning to see the problem for what it is. Americans in their teens and twenties, the so-called Generation X, know they will be overwhelmed trying to prop up the system for the older baby boomers just ahead of them, and they no longer believe they will benefit themselves. A 1994 survey found that a higher proportion of Generation Xers believe in the existence of UFOs than believe they will ever receive a nickel from Social Security.[9]

This all adds up to a prescription for social, political, and economic unrest. If we do nothing or if we respond to the worsening problem by raising taxes and cutting benefits yet again, the resulting generational conflict could pit father against son, mother against daughter.

Yet, there is a reasonable, workable solution. In this book we attempt to show how the United States can gradually replace the Social Security system—while fully guaranteeing full benefits to all Americans with a system that allows people the freedom to invest some of their FICA (Federal Insurance Contributions Act) taxes in financial assets such as stocks, bonds, bank certificates of deposit, and mutual funds, thereby ensuring full benefits to all Americans. History shows that these assets more than meet retirement needs at a fraction of Social Security's cost. Such a program can be devised and made to work in America and elsewhere. Already it has been implemented successfully in Chile, and it is being considered in other countries. Under our plan, financial security for retirees would be more certain, workers' taxes would be cut, and the nation's staggering unfunded Social Security liability would drop by 60 percent. Our three guiding principles would be met. To reiterate, those principles are the following:

❖ That the elderly are able to retire with financial security,
❖ That younger workers should be able to keep the fruits of their labor, and
❖ That the economy should not be unreasonably or unnecessarily burdened by achieving the first two principles.

Let us also state that we are talking in this book about the retirement benefit portion of Social Security. Under our plan, disability insurance and hospital insurance continue on as they are. Neither would be altered even slightly.

With the debate over Social Security now fully engaged, there is still time to plan and act wisely, rather than react hastily as the system begins its exponential decay a decade or so from now. Political and business leaders must seize the initiative before it's too late. Their constituents and workers are already demanding it. The time is fast approaching when the most threatened leaders will be those with no serious reform alternative to offer.

We have spent our careers building pensions and other retirement investments for individuals, institutions, and nations. What we are confronting now is a matter of budgeting, not for one year's income and expenses, but for everyone's future.

We write as sons and fathers. We remember our own parents' hard-earned and ultimately comfortable retirements, cushioned by favorable demographics and a Social Security system that worked because it covered a comparatively small generation of retirees, with income from a huge generation of workers. We recognize how deeply Social Security has left its imprint on our nation and our people. Through the decades Social Security has enabled tens of millions of Americans to live a dignified, secure retirement. It has been one of the most noble social programs in American history. But we also recognize that changing times and shifting demographics demand that we change if we are to provide an opportunity for a secure retirement for all Americans.

CHAPTER TWO

REALITY BEHIND THE RHETORIC

A T FIRST GLANCE, the middle-aged Florida couple seemed to be rolling toward a comfortable, even well-to-do, retirement. They had a condominium, a Ford Explorer, a Lincoln Continental, their own thriving business, and a household income averaging around $62,500, putting them in the top quarter of American households.

Yet, they were featured in a front-page *Washington Post* story, headlined:

BABY BOOMERS' RETIREMENT COULD BE A BUST, LIVING STANDARDS MAY DROP AS SOCIAL SECURITY ROLLS BULGE

"We have no pensions, only small IRAs [individual retirement accounts]—a few thousand each—and we're just starting a profit-sharing plan, but we haven't put anything in yet," admitted Beverly. Had

11

they been wasteful big spenders? Hardly. She and hus-
band Franklin put their spare income into their
school-supplies business, health insurance, and children's education. Like most small, family businesses,
however, theirs will lose most of its value when the
two people who built it, Franklin and Beverly, retire.
Of the future, the forty-five-year-old Beverly said: "I
most likely will be high and dry in retirement, with
almost nothing but Social Security."[1]

The couple is all too typical of America's massive boom generation—the nearly seventy-six million Americans who were born
from 1946 through 1964 and who now represent 29 percent of
the 1996 population of 265 million.[2] As a group, the baby
boomers have been too slow to save and invest for the future,
making them more dependent on the dwindling purchasing
power of Social Security benefits. But combined with the
smaller generation after them, their large numbers threaten to
drive the Social Security system out of actuarial balance, as the
Social Security Administration admits.[3]

In fewer than twenty years, the first wave of the baby
boomers will be collecting their gold watches at work and slid-
ing into retirement, including fifty-year-old Bob, a married sub-
urbanite from mid-America. He's a midlevel worker, a survivor
of company downsizing, thankful to be making average wages
as he enters the final third of his career. He runs six miles a day
and some days has trouble believing he's fifty. Yet he's old
enough to remember seeing Elvis in black and white on "The Ed
Sullivan Show."

And, while he prefers Elvis to the Grateful Dead any day, the
death last year of Dead leader Jerry Garcia was a curious wake-
up call for Bob and millions of other boomers. That, plus

reports on Social Security's ill health and Merrill Lynch studies on Americans' low savings rates, has boomers like Bob belatedly thinking a lot about Social Security and how best to prepare for retirement. The clock is ticking, and he knows it. But what to do? That's exactly what he and many contemporaries are not so sure of.

While Beverly and Franklin are real people, Bob is a composite. But Bob and the several other composites that we will meet from time to time over the course of this book are real in the sense that they are based on solid demographic, actuarial, and polling data. We will use the composites sparingly but where appropriate for illustrative purposes.

Bob was born in 1946, the first year of the baby boom. The year before that there were forty-two workers being taxed for each individual receiving Social Security benefits.[4] He began work in his early twenties. Instead of retiring at age sixty-five, which is when people now can retire with full Social Security benefits, Bob and other first-wave baby boomers will have to wait until at least age sixty-six, because of a measure enacted by Congress in 1983. If Bob were to choose early retirement—at age sixty-two—his benefits would be sliced by 25 percent.

When Bob is ready to retire, the estimated value of his payroll contributions to Social Security will likely have surpassed $200,000. It could take him a dozen years or so to get back in retirement benefits what he paid in Old-Age and Survivors Insurance (OASI) taxes. That's what Social Security's own data show for those retiring just ahead and just behind Bob.[5]

He's aiming to retire in 2012 at age sixty-six. His Social Security benefits would replace 42 percent of his preretirement income. That's about what the average retiree would receive from Social Security.[6] But Social Security also calculates that it will be in the red soon after Bob retires.

PAY AS YOU GO, COLLECT IF YOU CAN

Because of Social Security's pay-as-you-go financing, the boomers will not be drawing on the contributions that they themselves made. That $200,000 Bob paid in taxes will have been spent long before. Bob's retirement and that of his contemporaries will be financed by the taxes paid by younger workers and their employers.

And that's a problem for the boomers, for the younger workers, and for Social Security. A few years after Bob and the other first-wave boomers retire, around 2013 or so, Social Security will be running a cash-flow deficit that will grow rapidly as tax revenues fail to keep pace with the inevitable boom in retirees.[7]

Back in 1950, there were sixteen workers paying Social Security taxes for each person receiving Social Security benefits. But by 2014, there will be only 2.7 workers paying Social Security

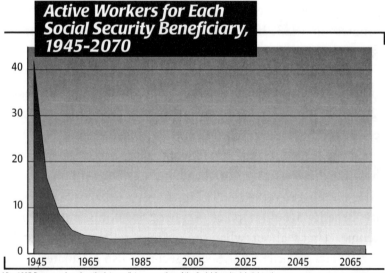

Active Workers for Each Social Security Beneficiary, 1945-2070

After 1995 figures are based on the intermediate assumption of the Social Security Administration. *Source: Social Security Administration*

Chart 1

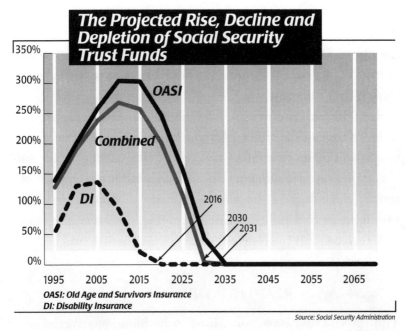

The Projected Rise, Decline and Depletion of Social Security Trust Funds

OASI

Combined

DI

2016

2030

2031

350%
300%
250%
200%
150%
100%
50%
0%

1995   2005   2015   2025   2035   2045   2055   2065

OASI: Old Age and Survivors Insurance
DI: Disability Insurance

Source: Social Security Administration

Chart 2

taxes for each person receiving benefits, down from the current 3.3 workers.[8]

By the year 2030 or so, as the last baby boomers approach retirement and the following generation enters the final stretch of their careers, there will be only two workers paying into the system to support each person drawing benefits. And Social Security's retirement and disability trust funds, which will already have been tapped to cover the earlier deficits, will be exhausted.[9]

These are not our forecasts. Rather, they are projections found in the Social Security Board of Trustees' 1995 annual report and summary. The projections are based on their best estimates of future demographic and economic conditions. But it could happen sooner. The forecasts have already become more pessimistic. Just three years ago, in 1993, Social Security forecast that its assets would not be depleted until 2036, six years later than the current predictions.[10]

While the funds are depleting, the numbers of retirees and those expecting to retire keep growing. Between now and 2030, the number of people entitled to Social Security benefits will skyrocket 86 percent or more; the number of active workers will grow only 17 percent.[11]

By 2030 Social Security will be running an annual cash deficit of more than $700 billion. After another five years the annual deficit will be more than $1 trillion.[12] Left unchanged, the system will keep pumping up the deficit without stopping. We simply will not have the money to cover our retirees without raising taxes to a politically unacceptable level, one that could sink the economy and leave the elderly even worse off.

A SACRED TRUST RECONSIDERED

This impending catastrophe, long in building, has stirred serious soul-searching in government and the private sector. In a series of hearings held last year by the Advisory Council on Social Security, appointed by the secretary of Health and Human Services, the governors and the governed glimpsed the reality behind the rhetoric. Among those testifying before the council's distinguished panel of elders and experts was Robert Lukefahr, a graduate student at the Wharton School of Business and a founder of Third Millennium, a young people's advocacy group formed in 1993 to sound the alarm on Social Security and other political issues.

"This is the lousiest investment a young person could make," said Lukefahr, who at thirty-one epitomizes what has been termed Generation X—the smaller generation that follows America's baby boomers.[13] Mr. Lukefahr's "lousy investment" observation is not just Generation X hyperbole.

During their work lives, Lukefahr's contemporaries will each

WHO'S COVERED

- ❖ Ninety-five percent of people age sixty-five or older at the beginning of 1996 were eligible to receive benefits when they or their spouses retired.
- ❖ Roughly 96 percent of jobs in the United States are covered under Social Security.
- ❖ The 5 percent not covered include (1) federal civilian workers hired before January 1984, (2) railroad workers, (3) certain employees in state and local government, and (4) low-income household, farm, and self-employed workers.

pay hundreds of thousands of dollars to Social Security in payroll taxes. "People of my generation pay these costs merely for the privilege of waiting in line for a retirement check that won't be there for them," he charges.[14]

Let's look at Social Security's own projections for three twenty-eight-year-old workers. We will call them Lou Low, Anne Average, and Max Most. Their names indicate their level of earnings, which in 1995 were $11,171 for Lou; $24,825 for Anne; and $61,200 for Max.[15] While Bob, the first-wave baby boomer, will be able to retire with full Social Security benefits at age sixty-six, these three young people will not qualify for full retirement benefits until age sixty-seven—another cost-saving measure by Congress.

By January 2035, when they attempt to retire, Lou will have paid $270,655 in Old-Age and Survivors Insurance (OASI) taxes to Social Security's retirement fund; Anne, $579,234; and Max, $1,454,147.[16] These estimates assume annual wage increases of 5 percent and annual interest on payroll taxes of over 6 percent.[17] Not included are the taxes that they also pay

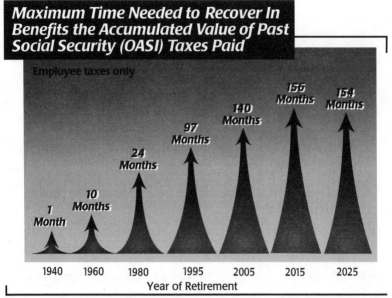

Chart 3

to Social Security's disability fund, hospital fund, or the matching taxes of their employers.

If Lou ever got to collect his benefits it would take Lou more than seven years to recover in retirement benefits the value of his OASI tax contributions; Anne, ten and one-half years; and Max, seventeen years, according to Social Security's calculations. In the case of Max, he likely won't live long enough to recover his investment. Contrast that with workers who retired in 1975—retirement benefits surpassed their tax contributions in two years or less.[18]

Unfortunately, Lou, Anne, and Max may not get their benefits at all. The 1995 annual report of Social Security's trustees says that under the current structure the system's trust funds will have run out of money four or five years before Lou, Anne, and Max attempt to retire. How could we ensure their benefits?

"There is, of course, always the option to raise taxes even further," replies Third Millennium's Lukefahr ironically. "The numbers have been clear for more than a decade. It does, however, beg the question: Does our nation really view its young people with such disregard?"[19]

PLAYING BY THE RULES

Yet, older Americans strongly and persuasively defend the system, contending that they have saved, worked hard, and supported the system, and now are entitled to its benefits.

"Those who say we can't afford to pay benefits to every contributor ignore the fact that Social Security is an earned benefit paid to retired and disabled workers, their families, and dependents of deceased workers," maintains John C. Rother, of the American Association of Retired Persons (AARP).[20]

Since trusting retirees have played by Washington's rules, how can one think of making them forfeit? We find it difficult to argue with our parents and grandparents, many of whom truly believe that their Social Security taxes were saved and invested in government trust funds for their retirement. Seniors also point, as does the Social Security Administration, to the three generations of American retirees benefiting from Social Security, an admirable achievement, indeed. And we certainly do not challenge today's retirees, nor seek to take away their benefits, nor blame them in any way. They have played by the rules.

Dorcas R. Hardy, Social Security commissioner from 1986 to 1989 during the Reagan and Bush administrations, offers a strikingly candid assessment of Social Security's strengths and shortcomings: "The current generation of retirees is enjoying a prosperity unknown to previous generations," which was exactly the purpose of the program. Unfortunately, she explains, such prosperity is "unlikely ever to return again. This prosperity does not derive from hard work and savings in years gone by. Rather, today's retired people are living on . . . people now working—the baby boomers in particular," wrote Hardy in 1991. "The way it's currently set up, Social Security is a lot like a chain letter—with the baby boomers holding the broken end of the chain."[21]

In earlier days, a stronger economy and fewer people drawing benefits disguised the system's inherent design flaws. Today between Third Millennium and the AARP falls the shadow of a stern economic reality: the system pits one generation against another.

When Social Security began collecting taxes in 1937, the worker paid a modest 1 percent on a maximum taxable income of $3,000 (equivalent to about $30,000 today), an amount matched by the employer. The rate covering just the OASI portion of Social Security (and not disability or Medicare) is now up to 5.26 percent on a maximum taxable income of $62,700, also matched by the employer. Through the decades Social Security has grown and expanded to the point where by 2002 it is projected that it will account for 22 percent of the federal budget.[22]

Even adjusted for inflation, the OASI maximum tax has increased almost 900 percent from 1951 to the present. During this same period Social Security benefits also increased, but at a much slower rate. The maximum retirement benefit in 1951 for a sixty-five-year-old worker was about $5,000 per year (1995 dollars). In 1995 it was $14,400, a rise of only 188 percent. Thus benefits received per tax dollar have fallen ever since 1951.[23] No matter how it's computed or by whom, the bottom line is the same: current and future workers, relative to taxes paid, will receive less, much less, in Social Security retirement benefits than did their parents and grandparents. There simply are too many people drawing benefits and too few paying taxes. As bad as this demographic mismatch is, it will only get worse.

SOCIAL SECURITY: THE BASICS

The system simply cannot be kept afloat at the present level of taxes and promised benefits. "During the past 5 years there has been a trend of deterioration in the long-range financial condition of the Social Security and Medicare programs and an acceleration in the projected dates of exhaustion in the related trust funds," state the trustees of Social Security and Medicare in the summary to their 1995 annual reports. The summary continued: "These adverse trends can be expected to continue and indicate the possibility of a future retirement crisis as the U.S. population begins to age rapidly. We urge that concerted action be taken promptly to address the critical public policy issues raised by the financing projections for these programs."[24]

The Clinton administration had already responded, appointing the Bipartisan Commission on Entitlement and Tax Reform in 1993 and, the following year, the Advisory Council on Social Security. Their hearings and reports underscored the extent of the crises and the dire need for genuine reform. Neither, however, was able to devise a unanimously endorsed plan, although other groups and concerned individuals advanced numerous remedies.

Many proposals to keep Social Security afloat have called for various combinations of increased payroll taxes, decreased benefits, means testing, and raised retirement age—even increasing immigration to get more workers paying into the system.

In 1994 then-U.S. Representative Dan Rostenkowski, the Chicago Democrat and chairman of the House Ways and Means

Committee, proposed legislation to cut cost-of-living increases in benefits, raise payroll taxes, and increase the retirement age beyond the increases already scheduled to take effect. While the legislation was never voted on, the fact that someone as central as Rostenkowski would have proposed such a package indicates the severity of the situation.[25]

A year later, in its report to the president, the Bipartisan Commission on Entitlement and Tax Reform cited as one of many options an immediate 2-percentage-point payroll tax increase. But even such a huge increase in the tax burden on workers would not solve the problem. "Even with an immediate 2.13-percentage-point payroll tax increase, the Trust Fund would run cash-flow deficits at the end of the seventy-five-year period," the Bipartisan Commission acknowledged. And that is assuming such an increase would not increase unemployment and thus reduce Social Security payments further. "Alternatively, payroll tax rates could be raised gradually over time, but that option would require a rise in payroll taxes of about 4 percentage points in 2030 (from 12.4 percent to 16.4 percent) to close the gap. Economists believe that the burden of payroll taxes falls largely on workers."[26]

In its 1994 report *U.S. Retirement Policy: The Sleeping Giant Awakens,* The Wyatt Company, the international consulting firm, concluded: "Even if half of the current shortfall is covered by increasing taxes, Wyatt estimates that benefits will have to be reduced at least 15 to 20 percent to bring the Social Security system into balance. Such changes must be made soon so that the baby boom generation will have time to adjust their other retirement savings in light of the more realistic (i.e., reduced) Social Security benefits."[27]

Factoring a rescue of the troubled Medicare system into the equation, the combined taxes on worker and employer to cover both systems could escalate to between 29 percent and 37 percent of payroll by the year 2020, warns the Concord Coalition, a citizen's lobby seeking to eliminate the federal deficit.[28]

There have been those who have proposed letting workers invest in their own private retirement funds. Variations of this idea have been discussed lately, typically calling for workers to continue paying taxes into the Social Security system while also being permitted to direct a portion of their tax money into private retirement accounts. That was one of the ideas proposed in 1996 by the Advisory Council on Social Security, although its members could not agree on just how to do it and how much to invest in private equities. At the same time, numerous members of the same Advisory Council also favored higher Social Security taxes and higher retirement age.

ECONOMIC BAND-AIDS

Social Security's sixty-one-year history proves that one more tax hike is never enough. Since the first Social Security tax was levied in 1937, Congress has raised the various tax rates more than twenty times. Taxpayers were assured that the tax hikes authorized by Congress in late 1977 would "restore the financial soundness of the cash-benefit program throughout the remainder of this century and into the early years of the next one."[29] But just six years later Congress was overhauling Social Security yet again, with a combination of higher payroll taxes; an increase in retirement age for baby boomers and younger workers; and a tax on benefits for upper-income retirees, in effect a reduction in their benefits. "The system does work," asserted Speaker of the House Thomas P. (Tip) O'Neill, Jr., when these new changes were signed into law. "This is a happy day for America."[30]

TAXES AND BENEFITS

- ❖ Currently, covered workers pay 7.65 percent of their gross salary in FICA taxes on earnings up to $62,700.
- ❖ Of this, 6.2 percent goes to OASDI and 1.45 percent goes to Medicare (Hospital Insurance, or HI). Employers pay an equal amount.
- ❖ Self-employed individuals pay the entire FICA tax of 15.3 percent themselves.
- ❖ Most individuals must work and pay into the system for about ten years to qualify for benefits.
- ❖ Eligible workers can receive reduced benefits at age sixty-two or full benefits at sixty-five. Anyone born after 1959 will not be eligible for full benefits until age sixty-seven.
- ❖ Social Security benefits are based on the best thirty-five years of lifetime earnings.

Not really. There are limits, both political and economic, on how much higher Social Security taxes can go. Let's take another look at the finances of Bob, the fifty-year-old first-wave baby boomer, and his wife, Barbara, a forty-six-year-old boomer. After finishing school, she pursued her career goals, as did other women her age. Now she's downshifted, as many women have. She works mainly for the second paycheck that she brings to the household. Barbara and Bob's combined income last year, $52,039, was the national family median. Of that, they paid fully 40.5 percent of their combined income in taxes, which included federal income tax, state and local taxes, and Social Security payroll taxes.[31] Their total tax bill was more than they paid for food, shelter, and clothing *combined*. They simply cannot pay more.

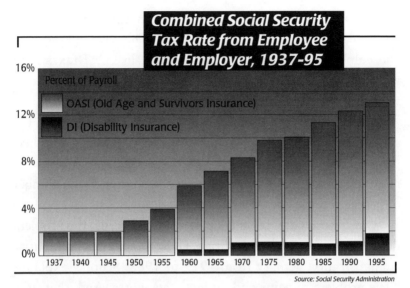

Source: Social Security Administration

Chart 4

Economist Carolyn L. Weaver, a member of the President's Advisory Council on Social Security, finds that "traditional tinkering with taxes and benefits just won't be satisfactory." Weaver, a scholar at the American Enterprise Institute, is the author of one of the seminal books on the subject, *The Crisis in Social Security: Economic and Political Origins,* published in 1982 by Duke Press Policy Studies.

She maintains that Social Security's looming deficit "stems from this pay-as-you-go system where we're promising a level of benefits and then trying to come up with a means of financing it. That's quite elusive in the face of the demographics we have."[32]

What tends to disguise the crisis and provides some with a dangerously false sense of security is the system's short-term surplus. In recent years the system's revenues have been pumped up by billions of dollars paid by workers from the baby boom generation, who are at or near peak earning power and represent one-half of the nation's workforce. This year, all workers and employers will pay $21 billion more in OASI taxes than will be spent on retirement and survivors' benefits. The excess will peak at $41 billion around the year 2008.[33]

But this temporary windfall will turn into a huge drain on the system as the baby boomers cease to be Social Security taxpayers and instead start drawing benefits. Will the system recover once the baby boomers have passed on and the number of people retiring each year becomes relatively smaller? No!

"Once those baby boomers pass from the scene, the problem doesn't go away," cautions Bruce D. Schobel, a Social Security Administration actuary from 1979 to 1988. Schobel explains, "The problem remains and, in fact, gets worse. And, that's the news! The reason it keeps getting worse is related almost entirely to life expectancy increases. The workers keep on living longer and longer, and the ratio of workers to beneficiaries keeps on dropping."[34]

In 1994 Social Security calculated life expectancy at birth to be 72.6 years for men and 79.0 years for women. It projects life expectancy to rise by about five years over the next seventy-five years—or by eight months each decade.[35]

By the year 2065 the child born in 1996 should be a few years into retirement—if there is still retirement. But by then retirees will live so long that there will be only 1.8 workers for each Social Security recipient.[36] These projections already assume net annual legal immigration of 650,000 and illegal immigration of 250,000.[37]

Thus, increasing immigration cannot possibly make up for the shortfall in workers, as some have suggested. Remember, immigrant workers become future Social Security retirees, entitled, themselves, to Social Security benefits. To maintain the 1990 worker:beneficiary ratio of 3.4:1 would require

110 million more workers than are projected by 2030 and 128 million more by 2050, according to a report by the Committee for Economic Development, an independent policy organization of business leaders and educators. Those added workers would represent about one-third of the projected U.S. population in those years. There is simply no way to bring about such a huge increase in the number and proportion of working Americans.[38]

TRUST FUND: A CONTRADICTION IN TERMS

We often hear that the current Social Security "surplus" is "invested" in the Social Security "trust fund" just as in an annuity or "insurance" program. All these terms, applied to Social Security, are government invented misnomers.

"Contrary to popular opinion, there are no special individual accounts—no shoe boxes with workers' names holding money in a Baltimore vault," says Dorcas Hardy, Social Security commissioner from 1986 to 1989.[39]

Workers are not, and never were, paying into personal, interest-bearing accounts like a savings account or IRA from which their benefits would be drawn at retirement. Nor does the government itself maintain a real trust fund.

Any surplus in the Social Security "trust funds" is not invested as are traditional trust funds—in diverse portfolios of earning assets. Rather, Social Security's positive cash flow is lent to the federal government, which spends its new source of funds on non–Social Security projects, such as bridge repairs, defense, food stamps, or whatever it chooses. In return, Social Security receives a piece of paper, an IOU. In reality, the federal government borrows money from itself. That's the household equivalent of paying off the MasterCard bill with a Visa advance. The homeowner still must pay. At the government level, the taxpayer still must pay.

THE TRUST FUND ILLUSION

❖ Social Security is a pay-as-you-go system; payroll taxes fund current benefits.

❖ For every dollar paid in FICA taxes, sixty-nine cents goes to retirees and their family members, nineteen cents goes to Medicare, and twelve cents goes to disability insurance.

❖ The trust fund is a bookkeeping account of how much money Social Security has received in taxes less how much it has paid in benefits. The difference is borrowed by the government and spent. Nonmarketable government IOUs represent this borrowing. They represent how much taxes will have to increase in the future to compensate Social Security for how much the government has spent in the past. This tax liability is presently $515 billion.

❖ When the fund goes into negative cash flow—where paid benefits exceed FICA taxes—the Treasury must pay Social Security back the money it has previously borrowed. Government actuaries estimate this will happen in the year 2013.

❖ In 2030 the trust fund itself will be depleted (the government will have paid back all it owes). At this point, Social Security will be unsustainable and taxes and benefits will be far out of balance.

"These bonds [IOUs] pay interest, and if the federal budget were running a surplus instead of a deficit, they would in fact constitute a reserve that could be drawn against in the future," notes Hardy. "However, because the federal budget is running a deficit of several hundred billion dollars a year, the Treasury will not have any cash on hand to pay off the bonds that Social Security is holding. In order to redeem the bonds, the Treasury will have to ask Congress to raise taxes."[40]

FOSTERING THE AGE OF ENTITLEMENT

Ironically, when introduced in the mid-1930s, one of the first official bulletins of the newly created Social Security Board reassured the American people: "The checks will come to you as a right."[41]

But there is no such right. The Supreme Court in 1960 ruled that workers have *no rights* to their taxes once they've paid them into Social Security. The Court ruled that Social Security's retirement program—OASI—"is in no sense a federally administered 'insurance program' under which each worker pays 'premiums' over the years and acquires at retirement an indefeasible right."[42]

More than two decades before the Court's ruling, however, the Social Security Administration in a four-page informational bulletin titled *Security in Your Old Age* concluded with these reassuring words: "What you get from the Government plan will always be more than you have paid in taxes and usually more than you can get for yourself by putting away the same amount of money each week in some other way."[43]

That was the rosy scenario in 1940, when there were forty-two workers for each beneficiary such as Miss Ida Mae Fuller, the recipient of monthly retirement check #00-000-001, for $22.54.

THE LONG LIFE AND LESSONS OF MISS FULLER

The historic check was hand-delivered to the sixty-five-year-old spinster and recently retired legal secretary living in Ludlow, Vermont, and duly recorded by news photographers on 31 January 1940.

Unlike today, the demographics were actually highly favorable at Social Security's outset. In 1940 the proportion of people aged sixty-five and older in the United States was only 6.8 percent of the total population, according to that year's census. Life expectancy at birth was calculated by the National Center for Health Statistics to be 63.6 years—61.4 years for men and 65.7 years for women. The Social Security system had set sixty-five as the age at which a qualified retired worker could begin to draw benefits. The hardy few who did make it to sixty-five could expect to live—and draw benefits—another dozen years (13.4 for women). With so many more workers than retirees, payroll taxes were expected to be low but paid by many, and benefits were expected to be high but received by few.

The reality, which demographers and actuaries have repeatedly bumped into, is that the present is markedly different than expected. Miss Fuller's experience, aided by Social Security, was both an endorsement for the fledgling system and a warning of future problems.

Known as "Aunt Ida," she received Social Security checks for thirty-five years. Living much of her retirement years with a niece, the Social Security figurehead once conceded that her monthly government check had "come pretty near paying for my expenses, because of living under one roof."[44] Not only was she the first benefits recipient, she also received the first cost-of-living increase in 1951, amounting to $18.75 a month. By then, the number of workers for each beneficiary had plummeted from forty-two to sixteen.

When Aunt Ida died on 27 January 1975 at age one hundred, a photograph and seven-paragraph obituary in the *New York Times* noted that she had received more than $20,000 in Social Security benefits. Her last check was for $109.20. Her total payroll contribution to Social Security was just $22.00. By the time she died, there were only 3.2 workers per beneficiary.

CHAPTER THREE

THE ORIGINS OF SOCIAL SECURITY

SOCIAL SECURITY WAS conceived amid the Depression as an effective and efficient way to protect older citizens—and others—from poverty and dependence.

Unemployment, which had been at 4 percent of the civilian labor force in 1928, rose to 16 percent by 1931, and jumped in the next year—a presidential election year—to 24 percent. In 1932 twelve million Americans were out of work—six times the number just four years before, according to Labor Department data. The stock market virtually imploded, free-falling 70 percent from Black Friday 1929 to 1935. Wall Street dealers and Broadway flappers were replaced by apple sellers and Dust Bowl migrants in the national image.

In March of 1933 Franklin Delano Roosevelt, the ebullient Democratic governor of New York, became the thirty-second president of the United States after soundly defeating Herbert Hoover, whom many blamed for the protracted Depression. Roosevelt promised "a new deal for the American people."[1]

31

Addressing Congress on 8 June 1934, Roosevelt took the offensive. He outlined his intentions for "rebuilding many of the structures of our economic life and of reorganizing it in order to prevent a recurrence of collapse. . . . Among our objectives I place the security of the men, women, and children of the nation first."[2] Toward that end, he would seek sweeping legislation dealing with housing, jobs, and what he called "social insurance"—a European concept more recently applied in America to government-legislated, tax-supported old-age pension programs, welfare, and unemployment benefits.

According to FDR, social insurance was needed not just because of the Depression's devastation, but because the tradition of mutual help and support among families and small communities was no longer equal to the economic crises of modern life in a large industrial nation. "The complexities of great communities and of organized industry make less real these simple means of security," he declaimed. "Therefore, we are compelled to employ the active interest of the nation as a whole through government in order to encourage a greater security for each individual who composes it."[3]

"GREAT DISTURBING FACTORS"

Roosevelt boldly pressed Congress for massive legislative action: "Next winter we may well undertake the great task of furthering the security of the citizen and his family through social insurance. This is not an untried experiment. Lessons of experience are available from states, from industries, and from many nations of the civilized world. The various types of social insurance are inter-related; and I think it is difficult to attempt to solve them piecemeal. Hence I am looking for a sound means which I can recommend to provide at once security against several of the great disturbing factors in life, especially those which relate to unemployment and old age. . . ."[4]

Other nations, particularly in Europe, followed developments in the United States with interest. One of Roosevelt's models for social insurance was Great Britain, where both Liberal and Conservative governments had instituted a widening array of programs in the first quarter of the century, beginning in 1908 with the nation's first old-age pension system, a noncontributory program providing financial aid to qualifying elderly poor. In layman's terms it was welfare.

Three years later the British government began offering workers' disability and unemployment benefits. In 1925, with the Conservatives newly in power, Parliament passed the Widows', Orphans', and Old Age Pension Act, a pension program that was supported by compulsory taxes on workers and employers.[5] By 1933 thirty-five countries had some form of government-run, old-age pension program.

Roosevelt's Social Security bill, which called for an array of welfare programs as well as a mandatory, tax-supported system of pensions for retired workers, was introduced by the Democrats in January of 1935. It faced some opposition and fostered rival plans. Critics warned it would cripple business, stall recovery, undermine the work ethic, and create dependency. One senator even warned that it could lower Americans "to the level of the average European."[6]

Others maintained the legislation didn't go far enough. The so-called Townsend Old-Age Revolving Pension Plan earned brisk press and public attention. The idea of a retired California doctor, Francis Townsend, it proposed paying $200 a month to all Americans aged sixty and older, with benefits to be financed by a 2 percent sales tax on everything. As if they were on some bulimic consumption binge, seniors would be required to spend their benefits within thirty days.[7]

POOR DEVILS AND RICH BIRDS

Louisiana's flamboyant populist social engineer, Huey ("The Kingfish") Long, elected to the U.S. Senate in 1932, also had a plan called "Share Our Wealth." Long proposed confiscating personal and family wealth over $4 million, raising income and inheritance taxes (100 percent on incomes over $1 million), and redistributing the income "so the poor devil who needs a house can get one from some rich bird who has too many houses." The rallying cry for Long's program was "Every man a king!"[8]

In the end, proposals such as Long's and Townsend's made Roosevelt's look modest in comparison, and the Social Security Act raced through Congress by votes of 372 to 33 in the House, and 77 to 6 in the Senate. The president signed the bill into law on 14 August 1935.

The act not only created the old-age and survivors' pension program that Americans have long referred to simply as Social Security, but it also instituted unemployment compensation and federal–state public assistance, while extending public health services, maternal and child health services, services for crippled children, child welfare, and vocational rehabilitation services.

Signing the bill into law, Roosevelt observed: "We can never insure 100 percent of the population against 100 percent of the hazards and vicissitudes of life, but we have tried to frame a law which will give some measure of protection to the average citizen and to his family against the loss of a job and against poverty-ridden old age. . . ."[9]

A BRIEF HISTORY OF SOCIAL SECURITY

1935 – Social Security Act signed by President Roosevelt.

1937 – Payroll tax first implemented.

1939 – Expanded coverage to include family members and survivors.

1940 – Payment of monthly benefits to retired workers begins.

1950 – States given the option to cover their employees.

1956 – Disability Insurance (DI) program added, providing income to disabled workers.

1965 – Medicare established: Part A established Hospital Insurance (HI); Part B established Supplementary Medical Insurance (SMI), which covers outpatient care and physician services.

1969 – Social Security moved on budget.

1983 – Social Security moved off budget.

1994 – Social Security Independence and Program Improvements Act removed Social Security from other economic and budget decision-making.

1995 – Social Security becomes an independent federal agency.

SELLING SOCIAL SECURITY

Social Security still had to be sold to the voters and protected against reversal by future Congresses. One sales technique was to use the language of insurance to promote the new program. Roosevelt thought this would make it more difficult, if not impossible, to change the course of events once he left office. The term social insurance was revived and used to characterize the fledgling system. "Admittedly, the Social Security Board [now the Social Security Administration] very definitely over-stressed the insurance concept in the early days of the program. This was done primarily to build up and maintain public support for the social security program—by drawing on the good name and reputation of private insurance," noted Robert J. Myers, Social Security's chief actuary from 1947 to 1970 and deputy commissioner in 1981–82.[10]

One of the first tasks of the Social Security Board, created to implement the legislation, was to explain its various benefits and obligations to the people to win their support and cooperation. To activate the old-age pension portion meant enlisting workers and employers to register and then begin paying more federal taxes—and this in the midst of the Great Depression. Following Roosevelt's lead, Social Security's architects and administrators chose their words carefully.

The Social Security Board's 1936 brochure, *Security in Your Old Age,* was filled with encouraging but inaccurate information. It said in part:

> The United States Government will, in the near future, set up a Social Security account for you, if you are eligible. . . . From the time you are 65 years old, or more, and stop working, you will get a Government check every month of your life. . . . The checks will come to you as a right. . . .
>
> Meanwhile, the Old-Age Reserve fund in the United States Treasury is drawing interest, and the Government guarantees it will never earn less than 3 percent. This means that 3 cents will be added to every dollar in the fund each year.[11]

After two pages of carrot, the brochure got around to the stick: payroll taxes, which later Social Security officials would generally call "contributions." But, despite the gentler term, Social Security payments, as authorized under FICA, are not contributions. They are taxes.

Social Security defenders from the beginning down to the present have tended to stress that workers pay only half the tax, with employers paying for the other half. In reality, of course, workers pay the entire tax, since employers offset the added tax burden by cutting wages or reducing total employment.

Retirees began receiving monthly Social Security checks in 1940. During the previous three years, small, one-time, lump-sum payments were made to some workers who had retired too soon to qualify for monthly benefits.

With a favorable Supreme Court ruling on the constitutionality of the system's old-age and unemployment provisions and with so many workers and employers paying into the system, Social Security's accounts grew rapidly. Some $416 million in payroll taxes poured into the system coffers in the twelve months ending in June 1939, while only $13.9 million was spent on lump-sum benefit payments and administrative costs.[12]

But this cornucopia of funds also threatened to create what has become a hefty—and handy—federal cookie jar. Senator Arthur H. Vandenberg (R–Mich.) and others had warned for two years that too much money was coming into the system and then being loaned out to the government, placing too great a future burden on the government to repay those IOUs with interest—the same argument that threatens to swamp the system today. The response of Congress set a precedent: spend it!

In 1939 amendments to the Social Security Act, which went into effect the following year, advocated spending money faster and on more people, thereby putting less in special government bonds. Among the changes introduced were monthly benefits originally set to begin in 1942 would begin in January of 1940, with "Aunt Ida" Fuller. More benefits would be added for qualifying family members and survivors.[13]

After getting Social Security up and running, President Roosevelt and Congress turned their attention to more pressing matters—getting planes, tanks, and ships rolling for World War II. Social Security went on autopilot.

What the president, Congress, and the nation could never have then imagined was that one of the results of the Allied victory was something that demographers and the headline writers years later dubbed the baby boom, which would eventually expose Social Security's fatal flaw.

CHAPTER FOUR

A GLOBAL CRISIS

FRANKLIN ROOSEVELT MAY have conceived of the program, but he didn't coin the term "social security." It was first uttered at a freedom rally in Venezuela in 1819 by Simon Bolívar, champion of South America's independence from Spanish colonial rule.

"The system of government most perfect is that which produces the greatest amount of happiness possible, the greatest amount of social security, and the greatest amount of political stability," proclaimed "The Great Liberator."[1]

Blending security and stability with happiness has proved a daunting task for governments, but Otto von Bismarck got a handle on the first two elements. The first government-run, mandatory, old-age pension system appeared in 1889 in Germany. Interestingly, Bismarck, its sponsor and thus the father of modern old-age social security, was neither a reformer nor particularly liberal. An aristocrat and autocrat, the Prussian "Iron Chancellor" advocated social security in hopes of pacifying the

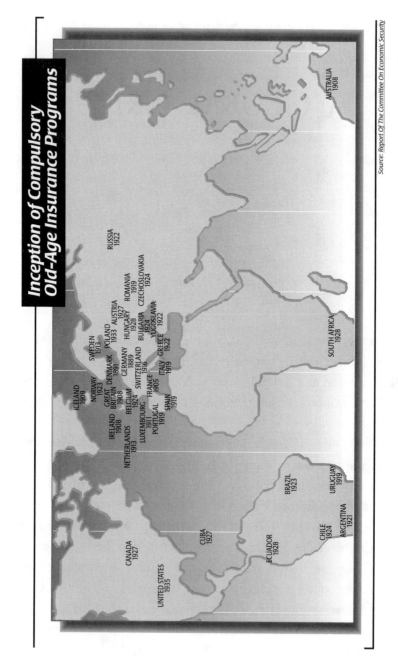

Inception of Compulsory Old-Age Insurance Programs

CANADA
1927

UNITED STATES
1935

CUBA
1927

ECUADOR
1928

BRAZIL
1923

URUGUAY
1919

CHILE
1924

ARGENTINA
1921

ICELAND
1909

NORWAY
1923

SWEDEN
1913

IRELAND
1911

GREAT BRITAIN
1908

DENMARK
1891

NETHERLANDS
1913

LUXEMBOURG
1911

BELGIUM
1924

GERMANY
1889

POLAND
1933

AUSTRIA
1927

HUNGARY
1928

ROMANIA
1919

RUSSIA
1922

SWITZERLAND
1916

FRANCE
1905

PORTUGAL
1919

SPAIN
1919

ITALY
1919

BULGARIA
1924

YUGOSLAVIA
1922

GREECE
1922

CZECHOSLOVAKIA
1924

SOUTH AFRICA
1928

AUSTRALIA
1908

Source: _Report Of The Committee On Economic Security_

Chart 5

40

proletariat and luring them away from socialism. "If the worker had no more cause for complaint, then the roots of socialism would be drained off," he remarked in 1878.[2]

Over the next four decades, more than thirty other nations followed Bismarck's lead and enacted various types of government-run, old-age pension programs. Other nations followed most of Europe: New Zealand, Australia, Iceland, Newfoundland, Uruguay, Argentina, Brazil, Chile, Greenland, Canada, Cuba, Ecuador, and South Africa.

Many of these pioneering pension programs and the variations that sprang up in more than one hundred other countries, including the United States, are today in serious financial difficulty, from the same problems haunting America's Social Security system: benefits and the number of recipients growing faster than the number of workers to support them.

EARLY EXPERIMENTS IN SECURITY

In nineteenth-century Europe—as in the United States—retirement as rest and relief was as mythological as Valhalla. With life expectancy below age fifty, most workers stayed on the job until they were injured, fell ill, or died. Retirement was to be feared as a time of frailty or ruin.

The Industrial Revolution—with its premium on strength, endurance, and speed in labor—devoured human resources. Age, infirmity, injury, and lay-offs dogged the bowed laborers of the new industrial age. Increasingly, workers and their organizations sought solutions to dehumanizing conditions of the "age of the machine" by combining strength and numbers in mutual aid societies.

England long served as a laboratory for various welfare initiatives, giving inspiration to other nations. Fraternal organizations, such as the Manchester Unity of Oddfellows, emerged from private sector concerns in the nineteenth century and offered members private life insurance, fellowship, and social and educational programs. Membership in "friendly societies" in Great Britain increased from 1 million in 1815 to more than 4.25 million by 1891—roughly half of the adult male population. For a weekly premium of four to six pence, members got medical coverage, death benefits, and sick pay, which averaged ten shillings a week.[3]

The private sector combined with government to fashion social safety nets. The British Postal Savings Bank Act of 1864 rewrote banking regulations to permit qualifying banks to underwrite life and old-age insurance.[4] In 1878 the Reverend William L. Blackley proposed the National Providence League to ensure the care of England's elderly and sick. Friendly societies opposed Blackley's compulsory plan, arguing it would undermine the habit of thrift. During the 1890s various committees set up by Parliament were again investigating the need for some sort of program to protect the elderly from poverty without destroying the work ethic.[5] By then, friendly societies had begun supporting mandatory programs, "owing partly to secessions from membership and partly to the failure of young men to join. Friendly societies were generally suffering from increases in demands for sick pay from members, particularly the aged."[6]

Meanwhile, mutual aid societies proliferated in France and elsewhere on the continent, offering members various insurance and social services. Outlawed during the French Revolution, societies reappeared after 1837, watched and regulated by government to quell potential subversion.

Proponents of the burgeoning voluntary sector associations believed that by pooling resources and investing reserves wisely, societies could provide their constituents with loans, accident insurance, and old-age pensions, as well as employment exchanges and medical care—without unduly burdening the state.

By the mid-1800s there were some 260 mutual benefit societies in Paris, typically affiliated with trade unions. One of the largest charitable and mutual aid groups in all of France at that time was the Society of St. Vincent de Paul, a Catholic group whose 30,000 members included artisans, clerks, factory workers, church employees, shopkeepers, and waiters, among others, in 1,300 branches. By 1852 some 2,488 societies in France boasted 239,000 members. Premiums were low, but so were the benefits. By 1900 the average pension was a mere seventy-one francs a year.[7]

"The French Republic must become a vast mutual benefit society," enthused French politico Paul Deschanel, who had long served as president of France's chamber of deputies before being elected president of the nation in 1920.[8] But despite rapid growth in the nineteenth century, the societies ultimately failed to deliver what proponents had promised. Too many were underfunded, mismanaged, or unable to attract sufficient new, young members to fund the needs of longtime members. Government attempts at subsidized insurance plans in the 1890s in France, Belgium, and Italy proved costly, unpopular, and ultimately short-lived.[9]

TRYING OUT THE OPEN HAND

Germany was shaken by a revolution in 1848, as was France, while rioters took to the streets of London. The unrest haunted Otto von Bismarck and convinced him he must *out-social* the socialists.

In Germany and elsewhere in Europe, socialists, as well as liberals and workers, had been pressing for sweeping changes in their lives of labor. Bismarck seized those issues for himself in a bold, triple-salvo, legislative counteroffensive in the early 1880s. First came his Sickness Insurance Law of 1883, then the Accident Insurance Law of 1884, followed by the Old-Age and Disability Insurance Law of 1889—a contributory old-age system similar to ours.[10]

Two years later Denmark instituted means-tested financial aid to elderly citizens in need, with benefits paid for out of general state and local revenues. The noncontributory program later was expanded to provide stipends to all older persons, regardless of income level or work history. Disability and sickness benefits were introduced around this time in Denmark and elsewhere in Scandinavia. Scandinavian countries, long the model of the modern welfare state, started out in the mid-1800s with the concept of "support for self-support."[11] But during decades of open-handed welfare the emphasis shifted steadily from self-support to state-dependency. Meanwhile, the region's tax rates soared to legendary levels, among the steepest in the world.

Nonetheless, various countries followed Denmark in instituting noncontributory old-age pension systems: New Zealand in 1898; France in 1905; Australia, Ireland, and Great Britain in 1908; and Iceland in 1909.[12]

Under the English system, people seventy and older received a pension of twenty-five pence a week, without having to go into a poorhouse to earn the money.[13] Young trade minister Winston Churchill, who helped push the Liberal government's 1908 pension proposal past Conservative opposition, confessed that he wanted to "thrust a big slice of *Bismarckianism* over the whole underside of our industrial system, and await the consequences whatever they may be with a good conscience."[14]

But, in fact, it was not so much Bismarckianism that Churchill thrust on industry's underside, as it was a variation of the Denmark plan, with the funds for the pensions coming out of the general taxes.

France opted for the real German model, a compulsory, contributory plan of payroll taxes on workers and employers to fund retiree benefits. In the next twenty-three years, a compulsory program clearly emerged as the preferred model, adopted by another twenty-four countries, including Romania, the Netherlands, Sweden, Italy, Spain, Greece, Russia, Belgium, Chile, Czechoslovakia, Poland, and Great Britain.[15]

Today virtually all of those systems are in as much or more trouble as the U.S. Social Security system. A quick glance at the demographic profile of twenty-four industrialized nations,

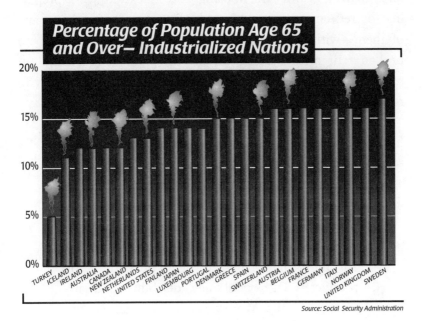

Percentage of Population Age 65 and Over– Industrialized Nations

Source: Social Security Administration

Chart 6

published by the Social Security Administration itself, begins to tell the story. Sixteen of those nations have higher percentages than the United States of people sixty-five–plus. Where 13 percent of the U.S. population is now age sixty-five or older, the proportion is 17 percent in Sweden; 16 percent in Austria, Belgium, France, Germany, Italy, Norway, and the United Kingdom; 15 percent in Denmark, Greece, Spain, and Switzerland; and 14 percent in Finland, Japan, Luxembourg, and Portugal.[16] What these percentages clearly indicate is that the pension systems in those countries face a crisis due to rising life expectancy, aging populations, and low fertility rates.

The situation is also heating up in many developing countries, where inflation, high unemployment, and weak economies have put their pension systems on alert status. The problem in the Third World is often put off by countries whose focus is on jobs, growth, health care, housing, and education, while preparing for retirement is far down the list of priorities. Yet many of them—with the advantages of young populations and no broken retirement systems already in place—could head off major dislocations later on if they paid some attention now to retirement.

In fact, a majority of the world's old-age pension plans are financially unstable. According to a thoroughly researched 1994 report by the World Bank titled *Averting the Old Age Crisis:*

❖ In 1990 the average member nation of the Organization for Economic Cooperation and Development spent 24 percent of the annual budget and more than 8 percent of its gross domestic product (GDP) on old-age, disability, and survivors' benefits. More was paid in social security taxes by the average citizen than in income or value-added taxes.

❖ Payroll taxes to cover pensions have reached 30 percent or higher in many Eastern European countries.

❖ Before reforms in 1994 each Argentinean worker supported two-thirds of a pensioner.

❖ The doubling of the sixty-plus population took 140 years in France, 86 years in Sweden, and 45 years in the United Kingdom. In China it will happen in 34 years and in Venezuela, 22 years.[17]

❖ Currently, 30 percent of the world's older people receive some sort of assistance from official old-age pension programs, and 40 percent of the world's workers who expect benefits at their retirement contribute to these programs. For most, the benefits will probably not match the taxes, yielding a negative rate of return.

❖ The sixty-plus population is projected to triple between 1990 and 2030, going from 9 percent to 16 percent of the global population.

❖ China, with one-fifth of the world's population, imposed a one-child policy to cut its rapid population growth. An unintended result of that policy is that by 2030, more than 20 percent of China's population will be over age sixty, dropping the ratio of workers per old person from 6 to 2.3 workers per retiree.[18]

The World Bank study, which was based on a two-year research project on old-age pensions around the world, reports: "Formal systems, such as government-backed pensions, have proved both unsustainable and very difficult to reform. In some developing countries, these systems are nearing collapse. In others, governments preparing to establish formal systems risk

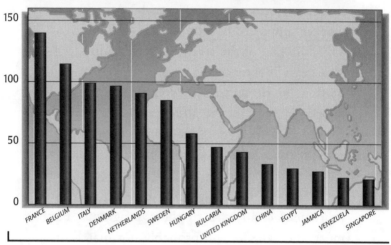

Number of Years Required to Double the Share of 60+ Population from 9 to 18%

Source: World Bank

Chart 7

repeating expensive mistakes. The result is a looming old age crisis that threatens not only the old but also their children and grandchildren, who must shoulder, directly or indirectly, much of the increasingly heavy burden of providing for the aged."[19]

This is certainly a gloomy finding, but there is hope. Chile, only sixteen years ago, had an old-age pension system nearing disintegration. The pay-as-you-go Chilean program, begun in 1924, had only two workers for each beneficiary by the late 1970s, with workers paying almost 19 percent of earnings into the program.[20] Tax evasion by workers was high, but so was the number of workers applying for benefits. And high inflation eroded the value of benefits.

Pushed to the brink of economic and social disaster, Chile successfully converted during the 1980s to a private old-age pension plan. Its investment component is sound, it generates strong returns, and it offers a valuable model for other countries. Numerous Latin American and European countries now are considering scrapping or scaling back their current systems for private pension systems such as Chile's.

MANAGING MYOPIA

Despite these encouraging signs, a myopia still dominates the fiscal future of social security systems. It is hard to avoid the notion that wishful thinking or vested interest has blinded those in positions to be effective watchdogs. "Many economists and policymakers are seeking information and advice about old-age security arrangements. But," the World Bank warns, "there are still too few who are aware of the impact these arrangements have on such diverse concerns as poverty, employment, inflation, and growth."[21]

CHAPTER FIVE

BOOMERS GO BUST?

THE DEMOGRAPHERS NEVER saw the boomers coming. In 1943 a team of experts released a forecast that the U.S. population, which stood at 132 million in 1940, would peak at 161 million by 1985 and then begin to decline.[1]

Because U.S. family size and fertility had been dropping for many decades, the projections seemed reasonable enough in 1943. But the modest, temporary uptick in births that demographers projected as returning World War II veterans settled back into family life wasn't the least bit modest or temporary. It lasted nineteen years, ratcheting births up to 75.9 million babies—all future consumers, workers, and retirees.[2]

Their sheer numbers made them instant trendsetters. And America, the culture, the economy, and Social Security have never quite gotten off the roller coaster. As one Census Bureau demographer with the benefit of hindsight puts it: "Society's attention is wherever the heck the baby boom is going to be. Whatever concerns a third of the population will be a major concern to our society."[3] In fact, the boomers, whose numbers immigration has increased to more than 77.8 million, represent 29 percent of the estimated 1996 U.S. population—still the biggest generation ever.[4]

America's baby boomers outnumber the entire populations of most nations, including the United Kingdom and France. Only twelve nations have populations outnumbering America's baby boomers.[5] In 1996 they are aged thirty-two to fifty and they span the most productive stage in the life cycle, at peak power in earnings and household consumption.

They are a generation to whom much has been given, a vocal generation that has demanded much and contributed much. They have repeatedly stimulated and transformed the nation and culture as they rampaged through many of America's once-hallowed institutions, fomented near-global soul-searching, and

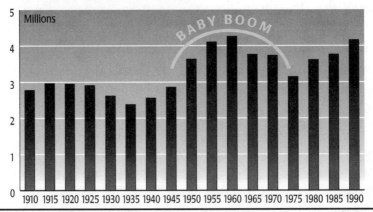

Number of Births in the U.S. 1909-1990

Source: National Center for Health Statistics and the Bureau of the Census.

Chart 8

scandalized their elders in tribal rituals such as Woodstock and Chicago's Days of Rage in an effort to define and discover their own independent, sometimes destructive, lifestyles. In the workplace, boomer men loosened their ties, boomer women pursued careers and wore slacks to the office, and together they imposed an informal atmosphere on the job, along with flextime and day care to accommodate their young children. They are still at it, this time redefining what it means to be, think, feel, and act middle-aged—a vibrant middle age, to be sure.

Just as they did with the culture, boomers from Day 1 and every day since have stimulated the economy, making sales boom—first in diapers and baby formulas, then Volkswagen buses and cheap airfares to exotic places; now in sport sedans, home products, Exercycles, Rollerblades, and weekend getaway vacations. As they look to and prepare for the future, they're also casting longing glances back at their youth. Their youthful demanding appetites and egos found meaning from Haight-Ashbury hippiedom to Silicon Valley high tech, and today it continues in a burgeoning nostalgia industry typified by golden-oldies radio stations, like New York City's top-rated WCBS–FM, that spin evocative songs from the 1950s, 1960s, and 1970s for the ears and dollars of wistful boomers. As *USA Today* has reported: "Rock stars will never die, they'll just become tomorrow's Frank Sinatras."[6]

While the music they enjoy may be laid back, the boomers were and are very competitive: They have to be competitive because of their vast numbers—wanting, needing, doing many of the same things at the same time. Boomers are forever bumping into one another—first in grade school, then high school, next in college, now the workplace. And, in less than two decades, it will happen all over again—at the branch offices of Social Security.

A look at grade school of the 1950s might provide a clue as to what's in store. Back then, more than thirty pupils to a public school classroom—thirty-five to forty kids in parochial schools—squirmed, often two to a desk, sharing books and supplies to stretch limited resources. Teachers somehow managed to maintain order, at least until the 1960s arrived. By then the boomers had learned to speak up and to "question authority," as the popular bumper sticker implored.

THE SOCIAL SECURITY BOOM

America's baby boom mirrored a boom in Social Security. Many of Franklin Roosevelt's New Deal programs, already well established, became an accepted—even expected—part of the political landscape. As the economy boomed and jobs blossomed, programs and benefits introduced during the Depression were extended. And new ones, such as the GI Bill and low-interest mortgages for veterans, created millions of instant, middle-class suburbanites comfortably raising their baby boom children.

Social Security also was revamped and expanded for more than two decades under a succession of both parties' administrations. During the Truman presidency, the Social Security Act was amended, extending mandatory old-age and survivors' coverage to some eight million more people who were not previously eligible, including the self-employed, farm workers, and certain educational workers.[7] Suddenly, eight million more people were paying into the system—and expecting to collect benefits later. Benefits were increased to keep ahead of inflation, while coverage was extended to Puerto Rico and the Virgin Islands. Tax increases were approved by Congress well in advance of going into effect as a way of ensuring that sufficient revenues would be produced to support the growing number of

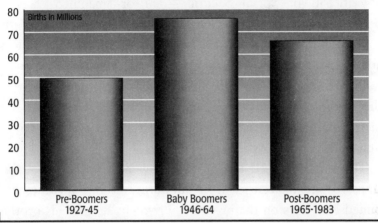

America's Baby Boom, Compared to Birth Cohorts Before and After the Boom

Births in Millions

| | Pre-Boomers 1927-45 | Baby Boomers 1946-64 | Post-Boomers 1965-1983 |

Source: National Center for Health Statistics and the Bureau of the Census

Chart 9

beneficiaries. The rate, steady since 1937 at 1 percent each on employee and employer on a maximum taxable income of $3,000, rose to 1.5 percent in 1950. The following year, the maximum taxable income increased to $3,600.[8]

FORGING THE "THIRD RAIL" OF POLITICS

How did Social Security become the sacrosanct, hallowed bureaucracy, dubbed the "third rail of politics"—an allusion to the electrified New York subway rail that was fatal if touched? The answer lies in its structure, franchise, and history.

Social Security created its own constituencies. As it extends benefits to more and more people, Social Security also breeds dependency and expands the constituency of beneficiaries who can be counted on to pressure any politician threatening the system. By 1950 the number of Social Security beneficiaries had grown to three million, almost triple the number five years before.

Criticism of Social Security—real or imagined—became political suicide early in the game, as Dwight Eisenhower discovered in 1949. Testing the presidential waters, the general advocated a strong, self-reliant America. Apparently referring to Social Security in a speech in Texas, Eisenhower remarked that the soldiers who fought and died in World War II "believed in something more than trying to be sure they would not be hungry when they were 67."[9]

The remark caused a furor. Eisenhower dropped critical allusions to Social Security from all future stump speeches and muted his views on the program. Privately, he told his brother Milton: "Should any political party attempt to abolish Social Security, unemployment insurance, and eliminate labor laws and farm programs, you would not hear of that party again in our political history."[10]

By the end of his successful 1952 campaign for the presidency, Eisenhower was vowing to cut taxes, rein in big government—and "improve and extend the federal program of Social Security."[11] During Eisenhower's two terms as president, Social Security benefits were authorized for disabled workers and for women taking early retirement, and old-age coverage was extended to clergymen and most state and local government workers.

By 1960, Eisenhower's last year in office, 13.7 million people were drawing retirement benefits from Social Security and another 522,000 were collecting the newly instituted disability benefits. There were then 5.1 workers paying into the system for each beneficiary. Payroll taxes had crept up to 3 percent on the worker and employer, each on a maximum taxable income of $4,800. The tax consisted of 2.75 percent going to the Old-Age and Survivors Insurance (OASI) fund, and 0.25 percent going into the Disability Insurance (DI) fund.[12]

ADDING CARS TO THE TRAIN

As John Kennedy succeeded Eisenhower, and Lyndon Johnson followed Kennedy, the tranquil 1950s gave way to the tumultuous 1960s. The first wave of the baby boomers was passing through high school and fanning out to colleges, the military, and the workplace. Congress and the White House—following tradition—kept adding cars to the Social Security train in the form of more benefits, more beneficiaries, and more taxes. The Social Security Amendments of 1961 extended early retirement to men at age sixty-two.[13]

Medicare, first proposed as a safety net for the sick by Harry Truman in 1945, was signed into law in 1965 by President Johnson.[14] Medicare's hospital benefits would be funded by piggybacking its tax onto the existing Social Security payroll tax— initially boosting it by 0.35 percentage points for the worker and employer.[15]

Social Security legislation passed in 1972 was further proof that presidents and legislators are expert in spending other people's money and passing the eroding buck, but not in regulating the Social Security system. During the 1972 presidential campaigns, Democrats proposed a generous 20 percent increase in benefits, which the Nixon administration initially opposed and wanted pared back to 5 percent. But President Nixon eventually relented, and the larger increase was approved, along with future cost-of-living adjustments (COLAs) in benefits tied to the Consumer Price Index (CPI). Also, significantly, the benefit formula for computing initial benefits was linked to both the national average wage and the CPI. This, now known as "double indexing," led to severe problems by the mid- to late 1970s.

In the waning days of the 1972 campaign, increase notices were sent to twenty-eight million senior citizens. Senator George McGovern, the Democratic presidential candidate, objected to the mailing, arguing that it "implies that the older people are indebted to Richard Nixon for that 20 percent increase. . . . [That's] very much like Scrooge trying to take credit for the Spirit of Christmas."[16]

FROM EXPANSION TO DOUBTS AND STRAINS

While the expansion of benefits long had politicians fighting to take credit, the inevitable tax increases that followed had legislators running for cover. By the mid-1970s the talk on Capitol Hill suddenly was no longer about adding yet more cars to the

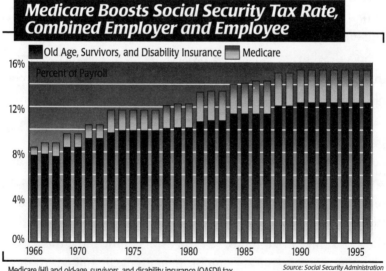

Medicare (HI) and old-age, survivors, and disability insurance (OASDI) tax for worker and employer combined (DASDHI) by year.

Source: Social Security Administration

Chart 10

train, but about Social Security's financial stability. Some quib-
bled at the size and length of the train, but others wondered
aloud if U.S. citizens were riding it or pulling it. The decades-
long explosion in benefits and recipients began to noticeably
strain the system's ability to pay.

In 1975 some 27 million people were drawing retirement
benefits and another 4.1 million were collecting disability, while
100 million workers paid the taxes to support them—only
3.2 workers for each beneficiary. Payroll taxes on worker and
employer were up to 4.95 percent each (4.375 percent covering
retirement benefits, 0.575 percent going to fund disability benefits). Many of the retirees were also among the nearly 20 million people eligible for Medicare's hospital benefits, which were
covered by an additional 0.90 percent payroll tax on worker
and employer.[17]

"Social Security: The Largest Welfare Program" was the
headline over an article by economist Jodie Allen that ran
6 April 1976 in the *Washington Post*. The article examined the
system's pay-as-you-go financing problems and redistributive
benefits formula. The hard-hitting report was something new—
sharp criticism of Social Security in a major paper, and it
brought about a powerful response.

Allen recalled the response this way:

> I was deluged by calls and letters from the guardians
> of the social security system . . . saying, "Gee, Jodie,
> we always liked you, but how could you say this?" I
> acted very politely, and I said, "Well, what's the matter
> with this; isn't it true?" And they said, "Oh, yes, it's
> true, but once you start saying this kind of thing, you
> don't know where it's going to end up." Then I came to
> perceive that social security was not a program; it was
> a religion. It's very hard to reform a religion.[18]

Though Congress went on to patch the system in 1977 and again in 1983, the real temporary rescuers of Social Security were the baby boomers, whose large numbers enriched its coffers. But the boomers, as we have seen, will be the system's final undoing as they begin retiring in another few decades, lining up for their own benefits and leaving the system bereft of once-heady payroll taxes.

CAPITAL-INTENSIVE LEISURE?

Bankers, brokers, insurance companies, and an assortment of telemarketers aggressively pitch investment opportunities to mature baby boomers, who are fast realizing that their dreams of comfortable retirement or capital-intensive leisure are in need of an early wake-up call. They are latecomers to saving, in addition to other pursuits. On average, they married roughly two years later than their parents and had smaller families—two children per couple. Boomers save a smaller percentage of their income than their parents did. Whereas their elders had thrift ingrained in them by the Depression, boomers' relative lack of thrift may result from growing up with doting parents buoyed to overgenerosity by postwar prosperity or the assumption that Social Security will be there when they retire.

In real terms, the average household income of boomers today is higher than that of their parents' at the same stage, but that income reflects a much higher proportion of boomer double-earners, a rising tide of working women. By the 1990s more than 70 percent of married women aged twenty-five to forty-four were in the workforce. In 1960 only one-third of married women in that age group worked outside the home.[19] The Census Bureau calculates that in constant 1993 dollars the median income for a married-couple household in 1993 was $43,005, versus $33,601 in 1967.[20]

But does more money buy a better life today? Boomers have more expenses than their parents had at the same stage in life. With so many mothers now in the workforce, child-care costs have zoomed. By 1991 one in four preschoolers of working mothers were enrolled in some form of organized child care, reports the Census Bureau.[21]

Factor in as well all the expensive gear that parents now find appropriate, if not essential, for their children's well-being, stuff that never existed in the 1950s—computers, calculators, CD players and compact disks, hand-held video recorders, VCRs and video tapes, Walkman radios and cassette players, Rollerblades, dirt bikes, crash helmets, $125 sneakers, and much, much more.

DOWNWARD MOBILITY?

It has long been an article of faith in the American Dream that each generation, through sacrifice and hard work, will do better than the preceding generation. And, for nearly two hundred years, this promise, in fact, has been realized.

The economic promise has reached far beyond mere creature comforts. The nearly mythic notion of continuing upward mobility has created expectations of unending personal improvement—the self-actualization movement in the psychotherapeutic seventies and eighties.

But the baby boomers, despite relative childhood comfort and higher education in this upward-and-onward era, could wind up being the first American generation to experience a declining standard of living.

Now, at mid-career, their passage thus far has not been smooth nor is it likely to improve. The last two decades dealt boomers at least four recessions and widespread business downsizing. Climbing the ladder of success has come slower for boomers than for their parents, and, as the ladder seems to steepen, it will be harder still for the second sitting of baby boomers—their way blocked by older boomers whose careers have already plateaued.

Nor will boomers fare as well as their parents did in owning homes or prospering from their appreciation. The escalation in value of their parents' homes was driven in large part by the demands of the pig in the python—their children. Boomers, who began entering the real estate market in the 1970s, tended to buy at the top of the market, paying much higher mortgage rates than their parents did. Demand from the generation following the boomers—smaller by several million—can't be as great.

TWO TO ONE: THE FUTURE TENSE

The implications of these trends for Social Security are troubling. In just sixteen years, by 2012, the first wave of boomers will begin to move into retirement. By 2030, as the first post-boomers approach that point, some seventy million Americans will be entitled to their Social Security retirement benefits and eleven million their disability benefits—after having spent their entire working lives paying into the system.[22] The numbers illustrate an indisputable dilemma—too many beneficiaries and not enough people to pay the benefits. The pay-in ratio will have sunk to just two workers supporting each beneficiary.[23]

Certainly, baby boomers will not retire as early as their parents and grandparents did. Already the age of retirement for boomers and the generation behind them has been bumped up between one and two years, depending on year of birth, as a result of Social Security changes in 1983. When boomers retire they certainly will not enjoy the level of Social Security benefits that their parents, grandparents, and "Aunt Ida" Fuller did.

There are just too many of them, and the generation behind them is too small.

This does not mean that boomers and younger generations cannot retire comfortably, just as older generations have. They can—but only if Social Security is fundamentally reformed. If it is not, they and those who follow will be crushed by the vice grips of demographics and the pay-as-you-go structure. This is the story of the dire need for real Social Security reform.

CHAPTER SIX

SAVING THE DREAM

BABY BOOMERS ARE woefully ill prepared for retirement. To retire comfortably, they must foment another revolution—this time in savings and investing.

In 1992 fewer than six out of ten American families had saved any money in the previous twelve months. And of those who did, only 27 percent cited retirement as the reason, a federal survey found. The most frequent reason mentioned for saving—cited by 42 percent—was "liquidity."[1]

After paying all the bills and adding up assets including savings, investments, and home equity, median net worth of American families stood at $52,000 in 1992—stalled about where it was three years before.[2] While not including future pension or Social Security benefits, net worth is an important building block in the retirement nest egg.

More than nine out of ten Americans do have financial investments of one type or another, but they are heavily concentrated in the more conservative instruments such as money market funds. There is no question that investing in the stock market carries with it a degree of risk, but even calculating in a reasonable degree of risk, the market has shown to be a solid investment over time. And as investors in recent years know so well, the market holds potential for substantial returns. Still, only 18 percent of all families and 20 perc nt of baby boomers are investing in stocks, whether individually or through mutual funds.[3] It will be very hard for Americans to increase their net worth as they did in the past with such paltry savings and low-return investments.

The good news is that asset accumulation and thus family net worth rises with age. For householders aged fifty-five to sixty-four, the median family net worth is $133,000 (1992 dollars).[4]

Still, those who track the trends voice concern, particularly about the baby boomers. "The typical baby boomer does not save nearly enough and will be forced to accept a significantly lower standard of living during retirement, or to delay retirement indefinitely, if his or her behavior remains unchanged," warns Stanford University economist B. Douglas Bernheim.[5] Based on his research for Merrill Lynch, Bernheim finds that "the typical baby boom household ought to nearly triple its rate of saving" to maintain its standard of living in retirement. They are now saving only 38 percent of what they need.[6] His calculations of savings and net worth do not include home equity, although 14 percent intend to use home equity to help finance their retirement; 60 percent view home equity as a source of security to be tapped only in a major emergency.[7]

The problem of low savings rates isn't limited to low- or average-income workers, or people unfamiliar with finance. Forty percent of retirement plan administrators were unsure if they themselves would have a sufficient nest egg at retirement time, and another 7 percent knew that they would not have

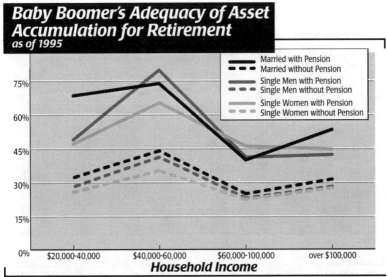

Baby Boomer's Adequacy of Asset Accumulation for Retirement as of 1995

Household Income: $20,000-40,000, $40,000-60,000, $60,000-100,000, over $100,000

Legend: Married with Pension, Married without Pension, Single Men with Pension, Single Men without Pension, Single Women with Pension, Single Women without Pension

Source: Merrill Lynch Baby Boom Retirement Index

Chart 11

enough, a survey of three hundred executives by CIGNA Retirement & Investment Services revealed. "They face similar college tuition and elder care cost pressures. Their focus is on today's cost of living, instead of imagining tomorrow's lifestyle and how to pay for it," says Thomas C. Carroll, Midwest regional vice president of CIGNA Retirement.[8]

SPEND NOW, PAY LATER

Boomers are just doing what comes naturally. They grew up in an era of prosperity and conspicuous consumption, were indulged by their generous parents, and are repeating the pattern. Most Americans have been on a spending spree for decades. It shows in the declining personal savings rate, which now hovers around 4 percent. Savings rates also have fallen in many other

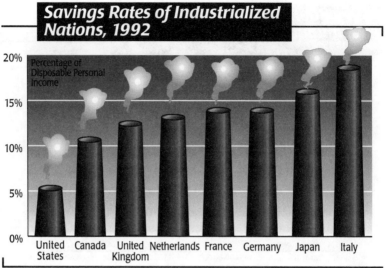

Source: U.S. Department of Commerce

Chart 12

countries in the postwar era, yet those rates remain two or three times higher than the U.S. level, generally because of tax codes that encourage thrift. In 1992 the savings rate in Italy was 18.7 percent of disposable personal income, followed by Japan, 16.0 percent; France and Germany, 13.9 percent; the Netherlands, 13.2 percent; the United Kingdom, 12.3 percent; and Canada, 10.6 percent.[9]

In contrast, American personal savings rates topped 20 percent during World War II.[10] The Depression hangover, the lack of available goods, and a spirit of shared sacrifice pushed wartime savings rates to more than double what they had ever been before or since.

Then, after decades of deprivation, Americans were ready and eager to spend. In the postwar period, savings rates were highest in the early 1970s—9.0 percent in 1973.[11] At the time, median household income was actually slightly higher in constant dollars than in the early 1990s. Government tax laws discouraged investment less then than now. By the late 1980s government tax policies were penalizing investment, and the savings rate slid to under 5 percent.[12]

By 1994 America's savings rate was a dismal 4.1 percent.[13] That year, four in ten baby boomers saved less than $1,000, a national poll discovered. In the same poll, 81 percent checked "yes" to the statement: "There always seems to be something else to spend on."[14]

An unusual eight-line headline over a 1995 front-page story in the *Wall Street Journal* summed up many boomers' perilous position:

BINGE BUYERS:
Many Baby Boomers
Save Little, May Run
Into Trouble Later On
They Don't Build Nest Eggs
Nearly Rapidly Enough
For an Easy Retirement
Still Longing for a Porsche

Journal reporter Bernard Wysocki, Jr., wrote:

Even the waves of corporate layoffs and declining real-estate prices that pummeled New England in the early 1990s haven't changed this free-spending bent. Conversations with southern New England boomers and people who know them—ranging from their auto dealers to their parents—show that many boomers are still dreaming big, materialistic dreams. . . .

"Today the fear is dropping a bit. The ones who have survived think they're OK," says Marilyn Steinmetz, a West Hartford, Conn., financial planner. "They want everything. They had it all. They still want it all. And they want it now."[15]

Yet, a few weeks before that article ran, *USA Today* profiled what it called "supersavers," including one forty-six-year-old payroll technician who said he saves almost half of what he takes home from his annual $30,000 salary.[16] He and others cited in the article, clearly exceptions to the rule, save the old-fashioned way—by living frugally, shopping for bargains, and resisting the temptation to splurge. These realists are fighting exasperating odds.

DISCOURAGING SAVINGS

Even thrifty Americans are being discouraged from saving and investing in several ways. For starters, right off the top of a worker's earnings comes the 5.26 percent tax to Social Security to pay for someone else's retirement benefit. Also not being invested is the additional 2.39 percent tax to Medicare and Social Security's disability fund nor the employer's matching portion.[17] From the get-go, Americans are putting 15.3 percent of their personal income into a plan that does not save anything. And Social Security demands yet more money—by taxing benefits of middle- and upper-income retirees. Social Security beneficiaries filing joint income tax returns are now subject to tax on 50 percent of their benefits if the combined income is between $32,000 and $44,000. For those with combined income of more than $44,000, 85 percent of Social Security benefits is subject to income tax.[18]

The taxes that discourage savings are far more pervasive. In addition to income tax, the U.S. tax code hits workers and retirees with a multitude of taxes—on savings and investment earnings, and the bequests that parents leave their children and grandchildren. While there are many ways to tax, there are too few incentives for trying to save. What tax incentives Congress can bestow to encourage savings, Congress can just as easily take away, as it did in 1986 in the case of Individual Retirement Accounts (IRAs) when deductions were reduced.

Add the Social Security taxes on top of federal income tax, state and local taxes, and assorted other taxes, and there's really only a widow's mite left over to save or invest. The typical two-earner family, with median family income of $52,039 in 1995, handed over 40.5 percent of that income in taxes, calculates the Tax Foundation in Washington, D.C. That's up from 27.6 percent in 1955. The single-earner family, with a 1995 median

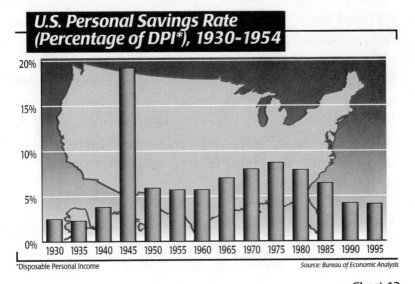

U.S. Personal Savings Rate (Percentage of DPI*), 1930-1954

*Disposable Personal Income

Source: Bureau of Economic Analysis

Chart 13

income of $27,788, paid 37.4 percent in taxes. That compares to 27.4 percent in 1955.[19]

"Saving and investing are so beneficial to the whole country and to everyone in it, including the government, that one would expect the government to encourage people to save and invest, or at least not to punish them for doing so," notes W. Thomas Kelly, president of the Savers & Investors League. "Incredibly, the government has designed our nation's income tax system to fall more heavily on income that is used for saving and investing than on income that is used for consumption." Kelly's group is leading a valiant charge for tax reform, spelled out in his 1994 book *Wealth Is Not a Dirty Word*.[20] In it, he points out the flaw in the current tax code: "If the income left after tax is used for consumption, there is no further tax (other than a few small federal excise taxes and a small sales tax in some states). If the after-tax income is saved, however, the return on the saving is hit repeatedly by another full round of income taxation by either the individual or corporate income tax, plus added layers of tax on dividends, capital gains, and transfers (gifts and estates)."[21]

Americans are trapped in a classic Catch-22. Social Security's high taxes lessen their ability to invest wage income in earning assets for retirement savings. People become ever more dependent on the government, the very cause of the dilemma. By the 1990s 63 percent of retirees are counting on Social Security for half or more of their income; one out of every four retirees depends on it for 90 percent or more of his or her income.[22]

THE PENSION OPTION CO-OPTED

By 1991 45 percent of private wage and salary workers were participating in private pension plans, many of which were facing the same demographic pressures as Social Security.[23]

And, amid cries for deficit reduction, politicians and federal bureaucrats are beginning to view private pensions, with their tax-preferred status, as an untapped source of revenue. "The United States has the ability to tax pensions on a current basis and the time has come to do it," wrote Alicia H. Munnell in 1992 when she was a senior vice president at the Federal Reserve Bank of Boston.[24]

Coverage and participation in pension plans vary markedly by age and industry, with those workers in their twenties least likely to be covered. Participation increases with age and job tenure, peaking at about 67 percent of the workers between the ages of forty-five to sixty-four, according to the Census Bureau's Current Population Survey. Segments underrepresented in pension plans are entry-level workers, part-time and low-income workers, and recently hired youth working at small businesses not offering pensions.

Some pension critics in and outside of Congress charge that the private system fails to protect the young and the disadvantaged, provides tax loopholes for employers, and largely benefits the upper-middle class and wealthy. Responding to such charges, as well as pension collapses of recent decades, Congress passed legislation designed to improve coverage and financial stability. But, as with Social Security, unintended consequences threaten the long-term viability of pensions.

DEFINED BENEFITS, DEFINED CONTRIBUTIONS DEFINED

The first pension plans in the United States predate Social Security by more than a half-century. The American Express Company set up a pension plan for its workers in 1875, followed by the Baltimore and Ohio Railroad Company in 1880. Another

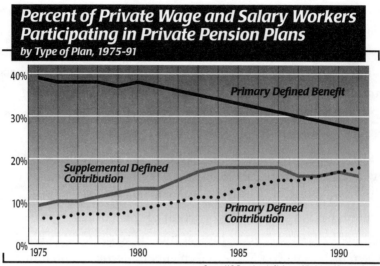

Percent of Private Wage and Salary Workers Participating in Private Pension Plans by Type of Plan, 1975-91

Primary Defined Benefit

Supplemental Defined Contribution

Primary Defined Contribution

Source: U.S. Department of Labor and the Internal Revenue Service

Chart 14

four hundred plans were established in the next fifty years, typically in the banking, railroad, and public utility industries, and then in manufacturing.[25]

Broadly speaking, there are two basic types of private pensions: a *defined benefit* plan and a *defined contribution* plan. A defined benefit plan provides a definite benefit formula for calculating benefit amounts, such as a flat amount per year of service or a percentage of salary times years of service. In this sort of plan the cost to the employer is determined actuarially as in an insurance policy. There are no individual accounts maintained, and benefits are defined by the program.

In a defined contribution plan, of which 401(k) plans are the most popular, the contributions are made to an individual account for each participating employee. The benefit amount is dependent upon the account balance at retirement. The balance depends upon the amounts contributed and the investment returns.

A BRIEF HISTORY

When America changed from a country of small family-run businesses to larger corporate enterprises—with long-serving employees—there developed a need for pension plans. As late as the 1920s formal pension systems were the exclusive province of a few industries: railroads, large commercial banks, and utilities. After World War II the number of pension systems exploded. There were two principal reasons: (1) passage of the Taft-Hartley Act that set forth statutory guidelines for jointly administered plans and (2) changes in federal labor law requiring that pensions be part of the collective bargaining process if requested by unions. Once employers established plans for their unionized workers, they set up similar or more generous systems for their salaried employees.

The majority of workers originally involved in pension plans were under a defined benefit formula. During the past twenty years, however, employers in the service and technology industries chose defined contribution plans over the traditional defined benefits systems. Defined contribution plans proved particularly popular with younger workers who liked the portability and self-directed features of these plans. The Revenue Act of 1978 allowed employees to contribute to defined contribution 401(k) plans on a pretax basis. Subsequently, many companies set up programs where they matched employee contributions up to a certain level. Some employers offer a combination of defined benefit and defined contribution plans to meet their employees' retirement needs.

DEFINED BENEFIT PLANS . . .
SOME BASIC FACTS

❖ Pension formulas are specified in advance and pay a percentage of the employee's annual earnings per year of service.

❖ Earnings are defined as the average salary over some period, typically the final three years of employment.

❖ Employers and sometimes employees pay into these plans.

❖ Contributions are invested by the employer and are used to pay future pension benefits. Employers bear the investment risk; employees and society assume the risk that the pension fund will become insolvent for economic or other reasons.

❖ Employees risk losing their pension if they change jobs.

DEFINED CONTRIBUTION PLANS . . .
SOME BASIC FACTS

❖ Employees contribute some defined amount into an individual account.

❖ These funds are invested as directed by the employee.

❖ The size of future pension benefits depends on how much money has accumulated at retirement and the number of years the employee expects to collect.

❖ Employees bear the investment risk as well as the risk that they will outlive their pension savings.

❖ Advantages of self-funded plans: (1) benefits are portable—they can travel with an employee to a new job; (2) they promote greater employee responsibility in planning for retirement; and (3) they offer opportunities for significant pension accrual, especially for younger workers.

LEGISLATING LOWER RETURNS

Of the two types, defined benefit plans have pursued more aggressive, far-sighted investment policies and have, on the whole, earned better investment returns than defined contribution plans. As recently as 1975, defined benefit plans covered the vast majority of workers enrolled in pension plans.

The tide shifted after passage of the Employee Retirement Income Security Act of 1974 (ERISA). ERISA, among its other features, guaranteed that workers would receive benefits if a defined pension plan were terminated. In other words, the employer would be held responsible if the pension fund went bust. ERISA established an insurance fund, into which employers paid premiums to guarantee worker benefits. Additionally, a minimum of 30 percent of the net worth of an employer was subject to a lien to cover any unfunded pension liabilities. There was no similar liability under a defined contribution plan.

Congress mistakenly expected that, with the protection of ERISA and the enforcement clout of the newly created Pension Benefit Guaranty Corporation, defined benefit plans would expand from their broad base to form the core of the private pension system. Unfortunately, ERISA made companies so fearful of defined benefit plans that the reverse is happening.

Many older companies have switched from defined benefit to defined contribution plans. Since the enactment of ERISA a large majority of employers starting pension plans have opted for defined contribution plans. By the year 2000 many experts in the pension and benefits field expect the breakdown to be 60 percent defined contribution plans and 40 percent defined benefit plans.[26]

The results? "Pension coverage has been diminished for a variety of reasons, particularly because of the shift in employment from manufacturing—where defined benefit plans traditionally were the rule—to services, with little if any pension coverage," observed AFL-CIO president Lane Kirkland, in a *USA Today* op-ed piece. "But there also has been an element of greed among employers who sought during the 1980s to limit their pension responsibilities. During the leveraged buyout frenzy of that decade, many employers raided so-called 'excess' assets from defined benefit plans without sharing one dollar with employees."[27]

There were, indeed, well-publicized pension fund raids, but the law has since been changed to protect against such activities. Most employers have acted responsibly and have simply responded to economics and increased competition, while trying to navigate through the minefields of laws and regulations. By cost alone, a smaller employer has little incentive to consider a defined benefit plan. In 1991 an employer with fifteen or fewer employees paid $455 per participant just to meet the regulatory costs of a defined benefit plan. For a defined contribution plan, the costs were roughly half that amount.[28]

From the employer's perspective it is easier, cheaper, and safer to contribute 2 percent of payroll each year into a defined contribution plan, whether it's a good year or a bad one, than to have to guarantee tens or even hundreds of thousands of dollars to a worker in twenty-five years under the elaborate formulas of a defined benefit plan, regardless of future business conditions.

Unfortunately, just as government was unintentionally encouraging employers to switch to defined contribution plans, other changes in tax and pension rules have penalized such plans. One dangerous and potentially devastating change in the government's accounting rules has encouraged employers to reduce contributions early in a worker's career, while increasing it as the worker gains seniority and advances toward retirement. Also serving to shrink the real dollar value of employer contributions has been a flurry of legislation, such as the Tax Equity and Fiscal Responsibility Act of 1982 (TEFRA), which cut the upper limits on contributions and benefits in tax-qualified pension plans. Benefits for top-wage earners, moreover, were capped to bring them closer to the average worker's benefit. The Tax Reform Act of 1986 continued TEFRA's limits by increasing restrictions on how much top-salaried workers could voluntarily put into 401(k) plans.

And finally, the Omnibus Budget Reconciliation Acts of 1987 and 1993 further dropped the ceiling on how much employers could contribute to their workers' tax-deferred pension funds. What all this means in real dollars and in the real world is that more money is exposed to taxation and less goes into pensions.

"Given the magnitude of the federal budget deficit, Congress has sought to tax pensions like any other form of income to 'capture' some of the lost revenues," noted a sobering 1994 report titled *U.S. Retirement Policy: The Sleeping Giant Awakens*. "But these efforts reveal an inherent dichotomy in U.S. retirement and tax policies: employers are encouraged to provide income security for their employees' golden years, yet employers are penalized by regulations that ultimately compel them to reduce their contribution levels."[29]

The report, which was produced by The Wyatt Company, warned:

In the not-too-distant future, corporate pension plans clearly will face the tough choice of higher con- tribution costs or lower pensions benefits, exactly the same prospect now facing the Social Security pro- gram. What will make this choice even more difficult is that many employers may have become too accus- tomed to the low contributions they have made to defined benefit plans in recent years because of regu- latory changes and the extraordinary performance of financial markets. . . .

What is particularly troubling is the possibility that the funding shortfalls of Social Security and employer- sponsored plans will occur simultaneously, forcing both systems to pare down promised benefits. That will leave the baby boomers in a tenuous financial position as they enter their golden years.[30]

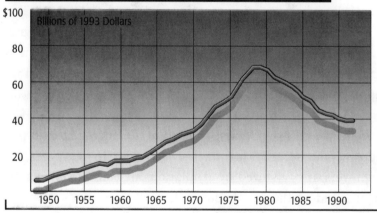

Employer Contributions to Private Pension and Profit Sharing Plans in Inflation-Adjusted Dollars, 1948-1992

Source: U.S. Department of Commerce and The Wyatt Company

Chart 15

Perhaps compounding the possibility of this double whammy for future retirees is the shift away from defined benefit plans toward defined contribution plans. While a defined contribution plan provides the individual worker more freedom with his or her money, it also imposes greater individual responsibility for investment results.

This double-edged sword falls directly on the baby boomers, a group used to making their own decisions on just about everything, especially what to do with their money. In the United States, the explosion of discount brokerage firms and directly purchased, no-load mutual funds (cutting out the broker) is a testament to this self-direction.

Yet, individual employees appear ill prepared, at least at the moment, to take responsibility for their own retirement funds.

Consider the implications of these statistics:

❖ Fifty-seven percent of participants in 401(k) plans do not contribute their maximum. With many companies matching, this means they are leaving found money on the table.

❖ One out of every four participants intends to use 401(k) savings for a house or a child's education—not retirement.

❖ Ninety percent of people who leave plans don't roll over their distributions into other retirement accounts and therefore lose benefits.

❖ Seventy-five percent of preretirees say they don't understand asset allocation: the percentage allocated to stocks, bonds, cash, etc. in an investment portfolio.

❖ Only 25 percent of preretirees say they understand compounding.

❖ Only 26 percent say they understand the effects
    of inflation.[31]

Given these numbers, it's not surprising that fully 64 percent
of 401(k) assets are invested in money markets, Guaranteed
Investment Contracts (GICs), or the employee's own company
stock. These investment choices, while easy for employees to
understand, are unlikely to generate the kinds of returns
required to fund a comfortable retirement. Such investments
are typically dependable, but too conservative and narrowly
focused. The investor choosing them must understand and consider a wider, more global range of investments and instruments
with historically greater returns.

CHAPTER SEVEN

BEARING THE BURDEN, SEARCHING FOR SOLUTIONS

T HEY GO BY many names—Generation X, the baby bust, 13th Gen, slackers, the grunge generation—none of which they've stuck on themselves. They think of themselves as the aftershocks, the kids born after America's baby boom. They take pride in not being boomers. In fact, asked if they would like to be like their elders, four out of five in the younger generation told *Fortune* magazine, "No way!"

So meet the post-boomers—the smaller generation born in America during the two decades after 1964.

In contrast to the 75.9 million boomers born during the period 1946 to 1964, there were only 65.9 million post-boomer births in America between 1965 and 1983.[1] Immigration, which has risen rapidly in recent years, especially in the wake of the 1986 and 1990 immigration laws, has added many more people to the post-boom group than to the boomer ranks, because disproportionate numbers of immigrants are in their twenties. Nevertheless, boomers still outnumber post-boomers and cast a long shadow over them. In 1996 77.8 million people are boomers, while 70.7 million are post-boomers.[2]

Many younger post-boomers see the baby boomers as a double-wide, oversized load always just ahead of them on the highway of life—a big eighteen-wheeler the younger generation will have to keep washed and fueled in later life. They have little faith that Social Security will be there for them.

Long eclipsed by more visible baby boomers, post-boomers are starting to challenge the status quo, asking tough questions and demanding real change. They are testifying before Congress, pressing their case through Third Millennium and other advocacy groups, outlining concerns in books like *Next: Young American Writers on the Next Generation.* They are mounting petition campaigns such as the "Lead . . . or Leave" drive, demanding that politicians pledge to cut the federal deficit or not seek reelection. You can hear them on MTV and read what's on their minds in magazines such as *Details* and *Spin,* as well as the op-ed pages of leading newspapers.

Testifying before the Senate Subcommittee on Social Security and Family Policy in June of 1995, twenty-four-year-old Heather Lamm of Third Millennium caught the attention of her elders when she declared:

> Is it fair to ask all of us to sacrifice in all areas of our lives to achieve a balanced budget in 2002, only to turn around and find a $600 billion bankrupt Social Security system knocking at our door early next century? . . .
>
> Mr. Chairman, no generation in American history has been left with the tail end of so many dysfunctional systems as the generation currently graduating

from college and entering the workplace. My peers and those after us will pay large amounts of our paychecks into programs that experts agree will be bankrupt by the time we retire. We are on the verge of inheriting a $5 trillion national debt, a crumbling national retirement system, decreased national savings, and an increasing number of retirees who expect to be generously supported. As a generation, we wonder how we can face this tremendous fiscal burden and still lead this nation into greatness. With boldness and clarity of purpose, let us seek answers together for the good of Americans today—and tomorrow.[3]

America's post-boomers, according to a national Third Millennium survey, are more likely to believe in the existence of UFOs

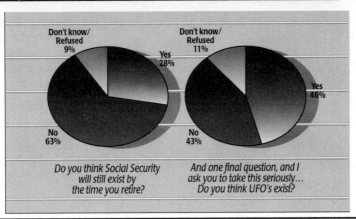

Proportion of 18 to 34 Year Olds Who Believe Social Security Will Have Money to Provide Them Expected Benefits, Versus Those Who Think UFO's Exist

Don't know/ Refused 9%
Yes 28%
No 63%
Do you think Social Security will still exist by the time you retire?

Don't know/ Refused 11%
Yes 46%
No 43%
And one final question, and I ask you to take this seriously... Do you think UFO's exist?

Source: Third Millennium Survey by Frank Luntz and Mark Siegel

Chart 16

than believe that they will ever collect Social Security. The poll, taken in September 1994, also found that 82 percent of young Americans want the freedom to invest a portion of their Social Security payments in private retirement accounts that they would control.[4]

These doubts about the system and a preference for doing their own investing reveal a keener awareness and concern than is found in the baby boomers, who have been slow to prepare for their futures.

"I plan to provide for myself and my family during my working years. Now the question remains: If I'm paying out so much of my gross salary in FICA, in taxes now, how am I going to accumulate wealth? That's an interesting question. That one I don't know. That could be a problem," remarks a thirty-one-year-old post-boomer acquaintance.

This young man also worries that the members of the baby boom generation will use their numbers and influence in the political arena to rewrite the rules of Social Security and other programs in their own interest. Even if nothing is rewritten, the boomers' retirement will clearly pass a crushing burden onto the post-boomers. In short, the careers and retirement prospects of the post-boomers are even more precarious than those of the boomers.

The possibility of generational conflict cannot be overstated. "If pushed to the edge economically, younger Americans, particularly people in their twenties and early thirties, would be the principal activists in this battle, taking to the streets and ballot boxes to demand immediate redress of their equity grievances," warn Jon Cowan and Rob Nelson in *Revolution X: A Survival Guide for Our Generation.*[5] In their early thirties, Cowan and Nelson are the founders of "Lead . . . or Leave."

THE CHADS, BRADS, AND JENNIFERS AMONG US

Traditional biblical names and basic Anglo-Saxon names predominate among the baby boomers: John, James, Peter, William, Paul, and David, and Mary, Elizabeth, Margaret, Christine, Catherine, and Anne, among others. But among the post-boomers in the late 1970s Jennifer came from out of nowhere to become the most popular name for a baby girl. And TV and Hollywood gave us a bumper crop of Samanthas, Jessicas, Laurens, Bettes, Clints, Chads, Brads, and Seans.

Brad Composite is twenty-eight; Jennifer Median is twenty-three. They are demographically typical Generation Xers. Despite his age, Brad is trying to finish his college degree part-time. He's currently in his third "real" job—a service rep in training at one of the smaller telephone companies that promotes its discounted rates. He's halfway through the six-month probation. It's not exactly what he wants, but it's okay, and they treat him fine, so far. The salary is average, the benefits are good, and there's a gym on site for employees. If the job works out, he might finally leave home to get his own place, which he's done twice before, each time coming back to the folks.

Excluding senior citizens, there's probably no age group more obsessed with Social Security than post-boomers. Social Security is one of those hot button issues that Brad and his friends talk and fret about.

While the Third Millennium survey didn't solicit his opinion, the organization's 1994 "UFO" poll captured Brad's view of Social Security. If he keeps slogging away in the marketplace, he would be entitled to benefits in his first year of retirement in 2035 of almost $66,000.[6] Sounds like a good deal, all right. But he knows that it isn't.

What the Social Security toll-free operator doesn't explain to Brad, but what he has ascertained from a little reconnoitering on the Internet, is that as an average wage-earner he will probably pay payroll taxes with an accumulated value of more than $600,000 to Social Security's OASI fund before he calls it quits.[7] And, that's not counting the additional sums he's required to hand over to the DI fund and Medicare. But, some two decades before he attempts to retire, Social Security will be running deficits. And, four or five years before he does retire, Social Security will have exhausted all of its so-called assets.

Brad wonders: "Why can't I relieve Social Security—and my fellow taxpayers—of the burden of caring for me in my old age and let me care for myself by letting me save for my own retirement? After all, this is America, isn't it?"

Jennifer, who just graduated from secretarial school, is at the start of her career, not counting the numerous after-school and summer jobs she had growing up. She's landed a position as an administrative assistant in a family-owned building supply company. As the chief assistant to the boss, she'll handle traditional secretarial duties, as well as record-keeping on the computer, with which she's quite facile. Assuming she remains in the workforce, she has four decades more of paying taxes into the Social Security system to fund not her own retirement, but benefits paid to people already retired, as well as the retirees, qualifying spouses, children, and survivors.

We have already seen how the crucial dependency ratio shrinks: 3.3 workers paying for each beneficiary today, 2.4 workers around the year 2020, and a disturbing 2:1 ratio by 2030. And, ten years after Jennifer reaches retirement age in 2040, there will be fewer than two workers for each retiree.[8] No wonder post-boomers worry.

"If no policy changes are made, payroll taxes must increase

to 24.6 percent by 2030 to support the Medicare and Social Security programs," warned the Bipartisan Commission on Entitlement and Tax Reform, in its January 1995 final report to President Clinton.[9]

Jennifer may not have a Ph.D. in economics, but she's wise with her money. She knows how to both spend and save it. That comes from years of helping her working mother run the household, from part-time "McJobs" during school to earn money for her canary yellow Neon, from watching Louis Rukeyser's "Wall Street Week," her favorite show after "The Simpsons," and from reading *Money* and other magazines that her mother subscribes to.

And, to Jennifer, Social Security doesn't make sense. Given the freedom to choose, she'd opt out of it. But, of course, the federal government doesn't give her that option. One option

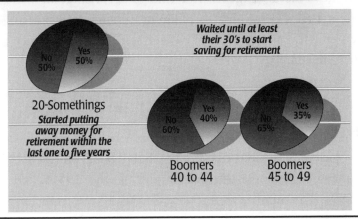

Comparison of Twentysomethings and Baby Boomers Who Began Putting Money Away for Retirement Nest-Egg
Last 1-5 Years

20-Somethings Started putting away money for retirement within the last one to five years — No 50%, Yes 50%

Waited until at least their 30's to start saving for retirement

Boomers 40 to 44 — No 60%, Yes 40%

Boomers 45 to 49 — No 65%, Yes 35%

Source: Kemper-Roper Retirement Monitor

Chart 17

she does have is the company 401(k) plan. While she doesn't earn much, she knows the power of compound interest, and the advantages that a private plan like a 401(k) has over Social Security. She intends to contribute the maximum allowable to take full advantage of the company match. She's not leaving any found money on the table. She may be only twenty-three, but Jennifer joins 58 percent of her contemporaries who are already putting money into 401(k) plans for retirement.[10]

Six out of every ten Americans in their twenties have already put money into savings or investments for their retirement. A 1995 survey, sponsored by Kemper Financial Services, Inc., also found that half of that age group started putting money aside for retirement within the past one to five years. In contrast, 40 percent of baby boomers aged forty to forty-four and 35 percent of boomers aged forty-five to forty-nine waited until at least their thirties.[11]

While 58 percent of those in their twenties had invested in 401(k) plans, only 52 percent of the boomers were in 401(k) plans at the time of the 1995 Kemper survey. "The so-called 'twentysomething' generation shows surprising sophistication about issues pertaining to planning, saving, and investing for retirement," says William E. Chapman II, executive vice president of Kemper.[12]

FROM BOOM TO BUST TO BOOMLET

The post-boomers were part of a great baby "bust." Then, just as society was adjusting to the baby bust, an "echo" baby boom—or boomlet—kicked in during the 1980s and early 1990s. The number of births and fertility rates shot up. Many baby boom women, who postponed marriage and motherhood a decade or two before, decided to start their families before it was too late. Even though they opted to have fewer children than their mothers had, the many more women in the baby boom generation ignited the temporary jump in births during the 1980s that made a dramatic contrast to the 1970s' low birth levels.

In the early 1990s federal statistics show almost one-third of all births were to women in their thirties.[13] Once again, demographers were surprised—not by the echo boom itself, but by its length and the high proportion of older mothers. The echo boom holds no promise for Social Security's problems, however. Inevitably, birth totals have started declining as, year by year, more baby boom women leave their child-bearing years behind. They are already being replaced by the post-boomers, which means fewer women entering into the child-bearing years, heralding an accelerated decline in births.

POST-BOOM HERITAGE: SELF-RELIANCE

As baby boomers were shaped by the tumultuous but indulgent sixties, so also are the two halves of the post-boomer generation yoked by their formative experiences. The post-boomers have had a large hand in raising themselves and their younger siblings, because their mothers were often at work. "In 1970, two in five children under age 18 had a mother in the labor force," notes demographer Suzanne M. Bianchi. "By 1988, three in five did."[14]

These are also the children of divorce. In her 1990 monograph, *America's Children: Mixed Prospects,* Bianchi reports:

> Since 1972, more than 1 million children each year have seen their parents divorce, a threefold increase since 1950. But the percentage of children whose

parents divorce has risen even faster. In the 1950s,
only six out of every 1,000 children experienced
parental divorce in a given year but in the 1980s, this
rate varied between 17 and 19 per 1,000. . . .

Because of the high divorce rate and the increase in
out-of-wedlock births, a smaller proportion of children are living in two-parent households. In 1960,
88 percent of children lived with two parents, but by
1988, this percentage had dropped to 73 percent. But
only about 60 percent lived with their two biological
parents in 1988; the remainder lived with a parent
and stepparent.[15]

Post-boomers not only have done the shopping and cooking for
their working mothers, they also have worked at earlier ages than
baby boomers, taking part-time jobs at fast-food restaurants or at
the mall while still in high school. They work to earn the money
to get what they want and need, including cars and college.

Thirty-nine percent of college freshmen expected to work to
help finance their schooling, according to a 1992 national survey by the Higher Education Research Institute at the University
of California, Los Angeles. The survey also found that one-third
intended to live with parents or other relatives during the school
year. Seventeen percent indicated that financing college was a
major worry.[16]

The prevalence of divorce and resulting increase in female-
headed households has forced many of the post-boomers to pay
their own way through college at a time when tuition has sky-
rocketed and course offerings have declined. Where the typical
student completed college in just over four years during the
1960s, students now take almost six years to get a degree,
because a higher proportion of those students are going part-
time and dropping out when they need to earn more money.[17]

While the worth of what's being taught in recent years is questioned by some, statistics show that post-boomers value and seek higher education even more than baby boomers. By the early 1990s more than 60 percent of high school graduates enrolled in college the following fall, compared to half in the 1970s.[18]

Yet even with their degrees and previous work experience, post-boomers have had a bumpy ride in the workforce so far, and it's likely to continue. Initially, in the mid-1980s, the older post-boomers fared pretty well, particularly in the service jobs. Filling in behind the more numerous tail-end boomers moving up and out of entry-level jobs, the post-boomers were in demand for a while. "As a result of a diminished rate of labor force growth and a smaller pool of qualified workers, particularly at the entry level, some employers may face skill shortages," wrote then-Assistant Secretary of Labor Roger D. Semerad in 1987. "Employers could respond to this situation by exporting jobs overseas, bidding up wages for qualified workers, investing more heavily in automation, or spending more for training and education of new employees."[19]

The marketplace advantage created by fewer post-boomers, however, proved discouragingly short-lived. It helped for part-time jobs and full-time entry-level jobs and perhaps a few rungs higher up, but recessions and corporate downsizing combined to neutralize their size advantage. Increasingly, post-boomers find themselves bumping into stalled boomers whose large numbers have impeded their own progress.

McJOBS: MAKING DO WITH LESS

As a result, some post-boomers wind up underemployed, in what author Douglas Coupland calls "McJobs" in his novel *Generation X: Tales for an Accelerated Culture*. Although written by a tail-end baby boomer, *Generation X* is a favorite with post-boomers who identify with the author's sardonic portrait of the young adult's obstacle course of life in the 1990s.

Many post-boomers eventually wind up in what's been called "new-collar" jobs. Definitely not blue-collar and not exactly white-collar either, these are the nonunion office jobs that have sprouted in one of the few sectors of the economy to register rapid growth in recent decades—the service sector, which now accounts for one-third of all U.S. employment. Since 1980 service jobs have grown more than twice as fast as overall employment.[20] These jobs include the myriad types of technicians who install, service, repair, and operate all the computers and electronic gear that are commonplace—if not essential—in virtually every business, factory, and corner grocery store. What distinguishes many of these jobs is the fair amount of high-tech skill required, coupled with mediocre wages and lack of vertical opportunity.

Research by the Economic Policy Institute finds that wages for young workers have declined for more than two decades. "We see [the declining living standard] in our McJobs, our shared living spaces, the declining value of our degrees and our bank accounts," write Cowan and Nelson in *Revolution X: A Survival Guide for Our Generation.*[21]

Yet inspiring post-boomer success stories are still aired in the financial press. "Computers Are Our Friends" was the headline atop a *Forbes* magazine story, profiling post-boomers who have already made it big in the world of commerce, computers, communications, and other fields.

As a generation, the post-boomers are not without their distinctive strengths in the marketplace. "The so-called Generation X is the most entrepreneurial generation in American history," reports *Forbes.* This is evidenced by the research of Marquette University's Paul Reynolds, who found that close to 10 percent of Americans aged twenty-five to thirty-four are actively engaged in launching a business. That's almost three times the rate of all other age groups.[22]

Being young and mostly not yet married, post-boomers have the advantage of lower wage demands. And, being the first generation weaned on computer game mania, they're much more adept at operating computers than their elders. Whether at McDonald's or on the corporate fast track, bosses have reported that post-boomers are, indeed, a new breed of American worker—independent minded, quietly questioning, and feisty, hard toilers from nine to five, yet protective of their free time and active in their social lives.

If they themselves weren't laid off during the corporate realignment, post-boomers know people who were. They're not expecting gold watches after spending twenty or more years with one company as dad or grandpa did. Besides, who'd want to? They sometimes come on with a chip on their shoulder but behave according to their own Golden Rule: treat them right and they'll treat you right. But they're not about to swear fealty to any company whose loyalty ends at lay-off times. Their jobs are important. They want to advance. But they're not the single-minded, cold-eyed careerists that so many baby boomers have become. Post-boomers are striving for a balance in all things. When it's quitting time, they have many hobbies and interests to pursue.

"These are the Employees Who Can Say No, a novel breed that won't be easily manipulated into workaholism by the traditional lures—money, title, security, and ladder climbing. Let's call them yiffies, for young, individualistic, freedom-minded, and few," suggested *Fortune* magazine. "The busters insist on getting satisfaction from their jobs but refuse to make personal sacrifices for the sake of the corporation. Their attitude: Other interests—leisure, family, lifestyle, the pursuit of experience—are as important as work."[23]

A Towers Perrin consultant told *Fortune:* "There's a real clash of values in the workplace right now. The old managers think that if the shoe doesn't fit, you should wear it and walk funny. The baby-busters say to throw it out and get a new shoe. Their attitude says that *they* are going to make the choices."[24]

The fresh breeze of their attitude, the entrepreneurial spirit, and the drive of post-boomers to make things happen will not only serve them well in the marketplace, but could also prove a catalyst to the nation in resolving the Social Security crisis that so directly threatens them.

DOWNSHIFTING VERSUS BOOMERANGING

The generation gap is back: "The new generation gap of the 1990s is different. It features a smoldering mutual disdain between Americans now reaching midlife and those born just after them. This time the moralizing aggressors are on the older side," reported *The Atlantic* in a 1992 cover story by two baby boomers titled "The New Generation Gap."[25]

Many critics have misread post-boomers, judging them to be whiners and slackers who shun responsibility and commitment—which naturally galls them. But a more empathetic insight was offered by Martha Farnsworth Riche, director of the Census Bureau during the Clinton administration, in a May 1990 *American Demographics* article. Riche, then an editor at the magazine, wrote:

> Move out, move in. Start school, stop school. Get a
> job, quit a job. Get married, get divorced. Young adults
> go back and forth like boomerangs. It's not because

they're spoiled or rebellious. It's because young adults face increasingly complex choices; they must investigate more options before they can settle into adult life.... Boomeranging is a rational response to changes in our society and economy. It is here to stay.[26]

Where boomers are busy trying to downshift, Riche finds that post-boomers are passing through a new phase in the life cycle, which she calls preadulthood. It involves sampling the options they have before committing themselves. They're proceeding cautiously, realizing, certainly more than baby boomers did at the same point in life, that choices—and mistakes—have real, often long-lasting consequences.

Fortunately, their vocal chords suffer no paralysis. Having found their collective voice in recent years, post-boomers speak up for themselves. They don't need or want anyone else interpreting them to the world or interpreting their world to them. After all, most are adults now and they have a big stake in large political issues such as Social Security, the deficit, and other public policy crises.

> We are devoted to cleaning up the mess left to us. Environment. Debt. Entitlements. Urban poverty. See a pattern? We do—it's a pattern of unfinished business and unintended consequences. When our time comes to call the shots, we will avoid that pattern. We will ensure that sacrifice is shared and burdens more equitable. In the meantime, young Americans are rolling up their sleeves and leading the cleanup.

So declared a manifesto appearing a few years ago in *The Next Progressive*, a publication written by post-boomers for themselves and anybody else interested in their ideas and issues. It continued:

> We are tired of the politics of false choices. Left or Right? Traditional or radical? We reject such made-for-TV dichotomies. Our ironic sensibilities are attuned to the ambiguities, subtleties, and contradictions in political life and public opinion, and so we take what works, whatever its ideological label may be. This is a generation in search of common ground, not new battlefields.
>
> We want to create change *now*. Just do it. That captures the urgent mindset of this generation.[27]

Since the burden of Social Security's financial crunch will fall most heavily on them, post-boomers are driven to find a solution for themselves. They may help to find one for all Americans. They're confronting the dilemma directly. While they may not have all the answers, they bear listening to. Their high rate of investment in 401(k) plans is encouraging and should be a lesson to their elders, particularly the baby boomers. They may wear their baseball caps backward, but post-boomers are definitely looking ahead. Whatever happens to Social Security, they must and will be key players in the debate and outcome of the program.

CHAPTER EIGHT

REFORM REDUX— FROM CARTER TO CLINTON

YEAR AFTER YEAR politicians on both sides of the aisle seek to assure us that one more patch job on Social Security's fraying fabric will do the trick. "From 1980 through 2030, the Social Security system will be sound," asserted President Jimmy Carter, on 20 December 1977, after signing a payroll tax increase on 110 million workers that was expected to raise an additional $227 billion in payroll taxes between 1979 and 1987.[1]

The measure was, at the time, the biggest tax hike in American history. *The New York Times* reported the next day that additional funds were needed to "eliminate a persistent excess of benefits over revenue."[2] In other words, a deficit. By 1979 payroll taxes going to the retirement fund were at 4.33 percent, and taxes going to the disability fund were at 0.75 percent, for a combined total of 5.08 percent on the worker and employer each. The maximum taxable income was raised immediately by almost one-third to $22,900.[3]

"This bill demonstrates for all time our nation's ironclad commitment to Social Security. It assures the elderly that America will always keep the promises made in troubled times a half century ago. It assures those who are still working that they, too, have a pact with the future. From this day forward, they have our pledge that they will get their fair share of benefits when they retire," said President Ronald Reagan as he signed the Social Security Amendments of 1983, raising taxes yet again.[4]

"Today," Reagan told a party assembled on the White House lawn, "all of us can look each other square in the eye and say, 'We kept our promises. We promised that we would protect the financial integrity of Social Security. We have. We promised that we would protect beneficiaries against any loss in current benefits. We have.'"[5]

The 1983 bill, meant to pump an additional $165 billion into the system by the end of the decade, was also the first to raise the retirement age and to impose taxes on benefits. Suddenly liable for a tax on 50 percent of benefits were those retired individuals whose total income from all sources exceeded $25,000 and married couples with a combined income of $32,000.[6]

These fixes, like those before, did not address the system's underlying flaws: the pay-as-you-go Social Security system cannot sustain itself because the beneficiaries are fast outpacing the workers who support them. More alarming, taxes coming into the system in excess of benefits going out are not invested for future retirees—they are spent on government projects which have no connection with Social Security whatsoever.

POSTPONING THE RECKONING

The quick fixes of 1977 and 1983 like those in decades past merely postponed the day of reckoning while increasing its costs. Unfortunately, our political culture focuses far more on the short run—a time frame of, say, two years—than on the longer term. The political leader with the vision to look forward twenty-five years or more is rare.

Helping precipitate the recent rounds of crises were the Social Security changes enacted in 1972. Legislation that year pegged COLAs in benefits to the CPI as the best way to protect beneficiaries from the ravages of inflation.[7] Unfortunately for Social Security's balance sheet, the COLA design was structurally flawed. Benefits were indexed to both wages and prices. Given that wages rise with prices, the formula double-counted inflation, accelerating the system's hemorrhage. Even though this error was recognized early on, it took five years to fix it legislatively. As luck would have it, the timing of the benefit adjustment was poor. It went into effect in the wake of a recession that rocked the U.S. economy from mid-1973 through most of 1974

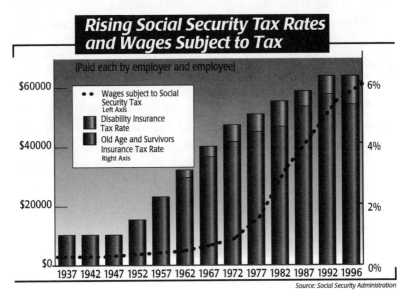

Rising Social Security Tax Rates and Wages Subject to Tax

(Paid each by employer and employee)

Wages subject to Social Security Tax
Left Axis

Disability Insurance Tax Rate

Old Age and Survivors Insurance Tax Rate
Right Axis

Source: Social Security Administration

Chart 18

and the OPEC oil embargo.[8] The COLA was further propelled by rising rates of inflation and unemployment that jumped from 4.8 percent in 1970 to 8.3 percent by 1975.[9] And later, it was discovered that the CPI formula tends to overstate inflation by 0.2 percent to 0.8 percent per year.[10]

By the presidential election of 1976 the candidates were courting senior votes not by promising boosts in Social Security benefits, but simply by promising to "rescue" the system.

In devising the 1977 overhaul, Congress and the White House had badly misjudged the timing and size of the eventual economic recovery and job growth. Just five years later the National Commission on Social Security Reform determined that $200 billion in additional financing would be needed to get Social Security through the 1980s.[11]

"Assumptions have often been too optimistic, partly because governments, for their own political reasons, use assumptions that are too optimistic," said a Carter administration economist years later in explaining what went wrong in 1977. "These are problems that are not unique to Social Security, and the problem with Social Security is only a symptom. Economists use models that are based on the past, and governments have encountered problems that they haven't encountered before."[12]

As the baby boom and then the baby bust have made abundantly clear to demographers and the world, the future frequently does not replicate the past, no matter what the experts project. If forecasters got things right in the mid-1940s, the U.S. population would have stopped growing years ago, or actually begun shrinking. Instead, it's growing by more than 2.5 million a year.[13]

Additionally, as Social Security has grown and matured with fewer workers contributing for each beneficiary, the system has become ultrasensitive to economic downturns, throwing budgets into chaos. When unemployment rises, even fewer workers pay taxes into the system. Yet the demand never slackens; it only grows, fed by an ever-aging population and inevitable CPI-triggered cost-of-living increases. The Bureau of Labor Statistics, which produces the CPI, has undertaken a review of its methodology in response to mounting evidence of the CPI's costly inaccuracy.[14]

SOCIAL SECURITY: AN APPEASEMENT STRATEGY

Not only did the reforms of 1977 and 1983 not deliver as advertised, but both the words and actions of the two presidents also were at odds with their earlier positions and comments on Social Security. Presidents Carter and Reagan were doing little more than trying to appease retirees on the one hand and workers on the other, while keeping Social Security afloat just a little while longer.

In his 1976 presidential bid, candidate Carter repeatedly rejected the idea of hiking the payroll tax as a solution to Social Security's woes. Once in office, he endorsed a payroll tax increase for workers and an even bigger one for their employers.[15]

Ronald Reagan had talked openly about the flaws of Social Security and, as far back as 1964, had warned of looming future deficits. And for years after, Reagan continued to warn of the problems with Social Security. He and his staff came to Washington, believing that they could truly reform Social Security—and do it the right way. Once inside the Washington Beltway, however, the message began to change.

"We had to withdraw a plan to cut billions of dollars in waste and fraud from the Social Security system—among other abuses, we'd discovered monthly Social Security checks were being sent to 8,500 people who'd been dead an average of eighty-one months—after the Democrats began accusing us of plotting to throw senior citizens to the wolves," recalled Reagan in his 1990 autobiography.[16]

HOWLING WOLVES: HELL TO PAY

Reagan hardly exaggerated. At the first hint of real reform, Democrats, organized labor, and a coalition of senior and labor groups called "Save Our Security" swung into action. They protested at the White House, on the evening news, in letters to the editor and their representatives, and in wave upon wave of telephone calls that swamped Capitol and White House switchboards, reminding the president and his staffers that Social Security was, indeed, a radioactive issue. On election day older Americans have the highest turnout of any age group.

Jim Baker, Reagan's chief of staff, got the message loud and clear. "My phones are ringing off the hook. I've got thousands of sixty-year-old textile workers who think it's the end of the world. What the hell am I supposed to tell them?"[17]

Office of Management and Budget head David Stockman wanted to forge ahead with reform efforts, but, "Jim Baker carried around a bazooka, firing first and asking questions later of anyone who mentioned the words 'Social Security.'"[18]

When it came time for the bipartisan rescue plan, Reagan, the conservative who came to office vowing to cut taxes, reversed field and agreed to tax upper-income retirees on their Social Security benefits.

Like his predecessors, Bill Clinton's words and deeds on Social Security have, over time, been contradictory. In a 1992 Macon, Georgia, campaign stop, he said: "We don't need to tamper with

Social Security. . . . We're not going to fool with Social Security. It's solid. It's secure. It's sound. And I'm going to keep it that way."[19] Once in office, faced with his first budget, President Clinton and his advisors seriously considered freezing Social Security cost-of-living increases and raising taxes on the benefits going to upper-income Americans. The measures were to be a part of Clinton's "share the sacrifice" deficit-reduction plan.

"That's a death wish and let's get it out of the way and forget it right now," said Senator Daniel Patrick Moynihan of the proposed COLA freeze.[20] Then-Treasury Secretary Lloyd Bentsen, a former senator from Texas, advised his president that fiddling with the cost-of-living allowance would be political suicide for legislators forced to support a freeze or cut.[21]

The mighty and persuasive American Association of Retired Persons (AARP), thirty-two million members strong, also protested. "Trying to mend fences at a White House meeting . . . , Mr. Clinton reassured . . . [AARP leaders] . . . that he considered Social Security to be a special contract with the nation's elderly," reported *The New York Times*.[22]

Less than two weeks later, when it came time to present the budget to the nation, the diet COLA had died, while a tax hike on benefits (which Bentsen insisted on calling a "spending cut" rather than a "tax increase") came through. When the president went before Congress and the nation, on the evening of 17 February 1993, he explained it this way: "The only change we are making in Social Security is [that] . . . the plan does ask older Americans with higher incomes who do not rely solely on Social Security to get by to contribute more. This plan will not affect the 80 percent of Social Security recipients who do not pay taxes on Social Security now."[23]

But to generate $21.4 billion annually in revenues, what he actually proposed was to up the ante for middle-class seniors, increasing the percentage of benefits subject to tax from 50 percent to 85 percent on the wealthiest 20 percent of beneficiaries.[24]

When finally enacted by Congress, the income threshold for inclusion of 85 percent of benefits subject to tax was raised to an annual income of $34,000 for individuals and over $44,000 for married couples.[25] The revenues generated by that increase are poured into Medicare's HI (Hospital Insurance) Trust Fund—in worse financial shape than the Social Security accounts.

Among academics, policy-makers, and elected officials, there is a clear consensus: *something* must be done. "I firmly believe that when the American public fully understands the entitlement dilemma, they will demand corrective action," wrote Senator Judd Gregg (R–N.H.) in an attachment to the final report. "Unless we act swiftly, the very programs that make

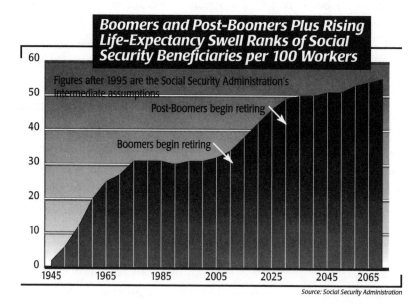

Source: Social Security Administration

Chart 19

congressmen and presidents most nervous about enacting reforms—Social Security and Medicare—will go bankrupt or confront severe benefit cuts."[26]

Seeking political cover, as well as politically acceptable solutions, Clinton in 1993 created the Bipartisan Commission on Entitlements and Tax Reform, and Health and Human Services Secretary Donna Shalala appointed the Quadrennial Advisory Council on Social Security in 1994. The thirty-two member Bipartisan Commission was headed by Senator Bob Kerrey (D–Neb.) and Senator John Danforth (R–Mo.). The members, however, were unable to agree on a unified action plan. Commission members presented five separate reform proposals by eight different members, with additional views by various commission members.

TO THE LIFEBOATS: S.S. RESCUE

After nearly two years of study and hearings, the thirteen-member Advisory Council on Social Security released its findings in 1996. We discuss the proposals offered by the council members in greater detail in chapter 10. What we find encouraging in the work of the council is that all three proposals recommend at least some level of private investment of Social Security funds.

Before the release of the report, Council Chairman Edward M. Gramlich, an economics professor at the University of Michigan, was quoted by *The New York Times* that "stocks have outperformed bonds by a significant margin over a long period of time."[27]

Advisory council member Robert Ball, who was commissioner of Social Security from 1962 to 1973, said: "Some of the trust fund money should be put into the stock market. I want to do it to get a better return for the Social Security system."[28]

An alternative floated by a few other members of the council is to require workers to contribute to private retirement accounts, in addition to paying their full Social Security payroll tax.[29]

For prominent members of a council appointed by a Democratic administration to reach the conclusion that private investment is needed to revitalize Social Security is a dramatic break with the past that fundamentally changed the nature of the debate about the future of Social Security. Even though there were assorted reform proposals advanced by council members and none was unanimously endorsed, the prominence given to private retirement funding, even on a partial level, makes the privatization concept acceptable for politicians of all parties seeking a promising solution to Social Security's inevitable crisis.

In addition to the reports of the Bipartisan Commission and the Advisory Council, several other serious proposals have been advanced recently by, among others, Senator Bob Kerrey and Senator Alan Simpson, who are working together on a series of bills; Steve Forbes, publisher of *Forbes* magazine and an unsuccessful candidate for the 1996 Republican presidential nomination; the nonpartisan Committee for Economic Development; and Third Millennium, the lobbying group of young Americans. And, from the other end of the generational spectrum, the AARP has also been heard from.

Many of these plans advocate some combination of benefit cuts and tax increases.

KERREY–SIMPSON PERSONAL INVESTMENT PLAN

Senator Simpson, Republican of Wyoming, was a member of the Bipartisan Commission on Entitlements that Senator Kerrey, Democrat of Nebraska, chaired. The two senators have joined together to sponsor a legislative package that involves some creative ideas that involve the private sector.

"Social Security is not a savings program. We'd like it to take on characteristics of savings in private pensions," says Kerrey.[30] His legislation allows investing a portion of the Old-Age, Survivors, and Disability Insurance Trust Funds in private equities to earn some real interest.[31]

The Kerrey–Simpson plan also would create a private investment account for workers, known as a Personal Investment Plan (PIP). Currently, a worker and his or her employer combined pay a total of 12.4 percent in OASDI payroll taxes on a maximum taxable income of $62,700. If a worker decides to join a PIP, two percentage points of the 12.4 percent tax could be invested in that person's individual PIP account. The worker has the option of choosing either a low-, medium-, or high-risk investment fund or putting the 2 percent into something like an IRA.[32]

Other features of the Kerrey–Simpson plan include raising the retirement age to seventy from its current sixty-five; holding COLAs to the CPI less 0.5 percentage points; and limiting COLAs for Social Security recipients whose benefits are above the thirtieth percentile of benefits paid.[33]

THE FORBES FORMULA

While the flat tax proposal was the main issue during his unsuccessful bid for the 1996 GOP presidential nod, Steve Forbes also had a plan to reform Social Security—let workers in their fifties and younger put a portion of their Social Security payroll taxes into stocks, bonds, or some other approved investment.

Qualifying workers would have their future Social Security benefits cut. In return, instead of paying the full amount of the

Social Security payroll tax, 1.5 percentage points from the worker and employer each would be redirected to private investments.[34] "People know there's a problem. And they like this idea," says Forbes.[35]

FULL DISCLOSURE AND OTHER LIFE RINGS

Level with the American people, advocates the Committee for Economic Development (CED), a nonpartisan research and policy group of some 250 business leaders and educators. Tell workers truthfully how much they put into the Social Security system and pension plans and how much they'll get out. Encourage them to start saving on their own. Reform the pension and tax laws to encourage private savings and widespread pension coverage, and make full funding of pensions mandatory. Above all, "no promises should be made that cannot be funded," says the CED in its 1995 report *Who Will Pay for Your Retirement? The Looming Crisis.*

"Steps should be taken to make sure that the building Social Security reserve funds do not serve to mask the non–Social Security federal budget deficit and that they result in an increase in real national savings," declared the CED, which also supports fully taxing benefits that exceed a beneficiary's contributions, a gradual trimming of benefits, and raising the retirement age.[36]

THIRD MILLENNIUM OPTION TO INVEST

Unwilling to sit back and leave the solutions to their elders, Third Millennium has jumped into the debate. A group of concerned young people formed Third Millennium in 1993 to protest what they perceived as "taxation without representation" in the towering national debt and programs such as Social Security.

"The American public, or at least people my age, now realize that their money is *not* safeguarded and invested in gold bars, real estate, or preferred shares of General Electric," states Third Millennium's Robert Lukefahr. "Without a genuine solution to this problem, young people will have no benefits to protect. If we do not sacrifice today, we will only increase our burden tomorrow."[37]

Third Millennium advocates a four-front assault: (1) means-test Social Security benefits; (2) tax 100 percent of those benefits; (3) raise the retirement age to seventy; and (4) cut back on benefits, and thus taxes, to permit workers to put a portion of their current payroll tax into individual retirement savings accounts.[38]

Support for Some Type of Personal Retirement Account Plan

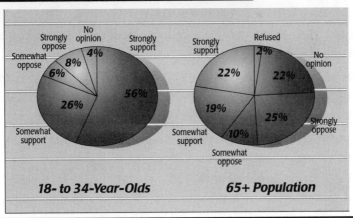

18- to 34-Year-Olds   **65+ Population**

Source: Third Millennium Survey by Frank Luntz and Mark Siegel

Chart 20

Proposal No. 4 got the high-five from 82 percent of young people, according to the national survey the group sponsored. A majority also supported means testing and taxing benefits.[39]

ADDING UP THE PLUSES AND MINUSES

The private investment features in many of these plans are a step in the right direction. The weakness in these plans, however, is that they provide incentives too weak to encourage the level of personal savings—and investment payback—needed to achieve financial security during retirement. But, more important, they remain wedded to the basic structure—and basic flaws—of the Social Security system, particularly for middle-aged and younger workers. They do not wean Americans from old-style Social Security, nor Social Security from its insatiable appetite for payroll tax fixes. Hiking payroll taxes hasn't worked yet, as the 1977 and 1983 reforms demonstrated, for tax increases have nothing to do with the fundamental flaws of the system. Though they can forestall the inevitable collapse of Social Security, they cannot avert it.

Yet all these proposals are encouraging because they acknowledge the problems, something long forbidden in American politics. Influential people, of all ages and parties, are getting involved and speaking out. The debate has begun and may embolden others to abandon the sidelines. All of a sudden real reform is not only a matter of national interest, but of political self-interest as well.

As Third Millennium's Lukefahr notes, "Doing the right thing—averting disaster—is also fast becoming politically expedient."[40]

At the other end of the age spectrum, even the AARP is subtly shifting gears, acknowledging problems and the need for remedial action. In recent years, and in the last round of debates on Capitol Hill, the thirty-two-million–member organization has come forward at least to critique various proposals others advocate.

"An early discussion of solvency options will allow workers and beneficiaries to voice their concerns and permit a full and open debate on possible courses of action," AARP board member Allan Tull told a Senate subcommittee hearing. "Social Security's long-term solvency can be restored by increasing revenue, reducing benefits, or some combination of the two. The last solvency package, the Social Security Amendments of 1983, included revenue and benefit changes. Sacrifices were asked of all who participate in the program: workers, employers, and beneficiaries—an approach that should serve as a model for the future."[41]

What's happening here? The baby boom!

AARP's constituency is "greening" with baby boomers, just now beginning to join its traditional base of members who experienced the Great Depression and won World War II. The oldest baby boomers are fifty this year, and despite its name, AARP membership is open to anyone aged fifty and older. Forty-eight percent of its thirty-two million members are already under the age of sixty-five. You can be sure that boomers will join AARP in large numbers and exert major influence within several years. Nothing can hold back this tide, as the grade schools, colleges, employers, and ultimately American society long ago found out.

Where once AARP viewed the baby boomers as the time bomb that would destroy the benefits of its members, AARP in the coming years will increasingly champion boomer interests. To paraphrase Walt Kelly's comic strip character Pogo, which might become AARP's motto in another decade or so: "We have met the baby boom, and the baby boom is us."

CHAPTER NINE

DIGGING OUT OF
THE SWAMP

T HE VILLAGE OF Escazu sits on a Costa Rican mountain-
top and commands a spectacular view of the capital city
of San Jose. Its residents live lives of simple pleasures,
enjoying clean air and mild temperatures, and occasionally
heading downtown for a movie, or a square dance at one of the
American clubs. Their neighborhood is nicknamed "Gringo
Gulch," because most residents are "pensionados"—retired
Americans who found a way to stretch their pension dollars in
paradise.

The Social Security Administration sends monthly checks
to 360,000 retirees and other beneficiaries living outside the
United States—2,100 in Costa Rica alone and another 56,000
in Mexico.[1] These folks have found a livable if occasionally
lonely solution to their personal Social Security crisis.

Many foreign countries welcome Americans with U.S. pension dollars to spend, especially since they do not add to their
host's own pension burden. Throughout the world, nations are

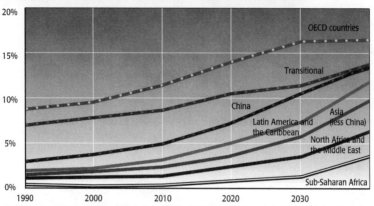

Projected Public Pension Spending as a Percentage of GPD, 1990-2050

OECD Countries: Australia, Austria, Belgium, Canada, Denmark, Finland, France, Germany, Greece, Iceland, Ireland, Italy, Japan, Luxembourg, Netherlands, New Zealand, Norway, Portugal, Spain, Sweden, Switzerland, Turkey, United Kingdom, United States

Source: Palacios and the World Bank

Chart 21

being overwhelmed by the costly IOUs covering unfunded pension liabilities. Most countries continue responding with the now familiar prescription of increased taxes and lowered benefits—temporary fixes that augment the pain and only skirt the disease.

But several countries—Australia, Britain, Chile, and Italy, to name but four—are undertaking bold, new initiatives to turn old-style Social Security into genuine savings and investment plans that boost both retirement benefits and the economy.

THE PRIVATE SECTOR RECONSIDERED

The private sector was rejected by the earliest social insurance advocates from Bismarck to Roosevelt as inadequate to the challenge of providing financial protection to older people. Today alternative privatized plans are being hotly debated in international circles. New plans involving private investment are emerging in several nations. They seek not only to relieve governments of their crushing pension burdens, but also to encourage capital formation, stimulate sluggish economies, and create jobs. Usually, they involve personal accounts for workers at privately run banks or insurance companies that function as pension fund administrators investing payroll taxes. Thus workers can invest in personal growth accounts and build assets for their own futures—unlike pay-as-you-go systems in which active workers fund retirees and government deficits.

Advocates say private systems reinforce the vital savings habit, the key to capital formation: money that workers put into their personal accounts is invested by the fund managers in manufacturing, research and development, construction, and other productive enterprises that ultimately can create wealth and jobs.

"In countries with relatively underdeveloped capital markets, like Chile's ten years ago, privatized pension fund savings played the major role in developing large, liquid pools of capital and in creating equity markets. . . . Capital market benefits can be important even in highly developed economies," reported the *Benefits Quarterly* journal in 1995. "A goal of Italy's recent retirement savings initiatives was to help bolster the country's underdeveloped stock market. . . . Similarly, France's planned shift toward private pensions is expected to produce a significant new source of funds for the stock market."[2]

"The case for switching has lately been endorsed by the likely victor in France's presidential election, by Germany's central bank, by the government of Italy, which is poised to enact a new pension law, and by many smaller countries," reported *The Economist* in mid-1995.

"On one estimate savings in pension funds could grow

fourfold over the next twenty-five years. . . . This mountain of money could change the financial landscape in Europe, boosting the growth of stock markets, increasing shareholder pressure on firms to perform well and making it easier for companies to finance investment."[3]

THE CHICAGO BOYS FROM CHILE

When the rescue team collectively known as the Chicago Boys was turned loose, Chile's pension system was in the late stages of hypertension, heading for a debilitating stroke. Launched in 1924 and the oldest in the Western Hemisphere, it had been balkanized by the 1970s into fifty-six separate funds for different industries and occupational groups, all pay-as-you-go with different retirement ages and different levels of benefits.

"The name of the game became pressure politics," explains Chilean economist Jose Pinera, an architect of the reformed system. "By pressuring Congress, each group of workers tried to minimize what it put in and maximize what it took out. For example, some groups were able to reduce their members' retirement age, thereby getting them their benefits sooner, at the expense of those who had to work longer.

"The result was a labyrinth of different and unfair pension provisions, with some powerful groups able to retire their members with nearly full benefits after as few as 25 years of work."[4]

Evasion of payroll taxes in Chile ran as high as 30 percent. Workers and employers routinely underreported earnings to lower the taxes they paid until five years before retirement, the period used to calculate final benefits. The ratio of workers to beneficiaries had dropped to only 2.2 to 1. By 1981 Chile's sprawling Social Security system was running a deficit of 28 percent.[5]

Faced with the system's near collapse, General Augusto Pinochet Ugarte turned to a team of young Chilean economists, mostly graduates of the University of Chicago, famed citadel of free-market economics. Jose Pinera, the exception, earned his Ph.D. at Harvard. Pension reform was the first part of a larger overhaul of Chile's economy, which included privatizing government airline, steel, and utility companies. In accordance with their plan, the government-run pension system in mid-1981 began the transition to a privately administered, national system of mandatory retirement savings.

The new pension program authorized private companies known as Pension Fund Administrators, or *Administradoras de Fondos de Pensiones* in Spanish, and commonly referred to as AFPs. Workers joining the system were required to save 10 percent of their wages in individual investment accounts at the AFP. The AFPs in turn invested the money in diversified portfolios. Workers could elect to withhold up to 20 percent of earnings. For the first two years, workers already in the labor force could choose to remain with the old system, which older workers tended to do, or join an AFP. After that point, new workers were required to join the new system.[6]

SWITCHING TO A NEW TRACK

For the transition to succeed, the Chicago Boys had to satisfy two key workers' concerns that will likely confront any country switching to a similar new track: (1) If a worker transfers to the new system, what happens to the contributions that he made to the old system? (2) As active workers leave the old, government-run system and payroll taxes therefore decline, how will that system pay the benefits of the retirees electing to stay with that system?

In Chile, each worker who switched to the private system received a treasury bond, known as a recognition bond, from the government that credited the worker for past contributions to the old system. The recognition bond, which matured upon the holder's retirement, promised a government-guaranteed real rate of return of 4 percent a year, which was also the minimum rate required of AFPs.[7]

For those opting to remain in the old system, benefits would continue to be paid from payroll taxes, proceeds from the sale of state-run industries, and general revenues.

"The bottom line is that when given the choice, workers will vote with their money overwhelmingly for the free market— even when it comes to such sacred cows as Social Security. And the free market has not let them down," contends Pinera.[8]

Ninety percent of Chile's eligible workers chose to leave the government program and join the private AFP system. Those

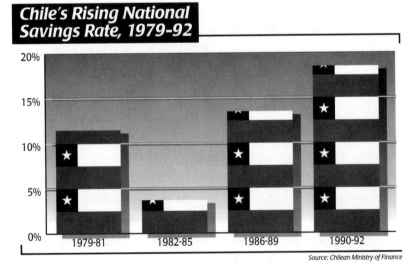

Chile's Rising National Savings Rate, 1979-92

Source: Chilean Ministry of Finance

Chart 22

who stuck with the old system are paying 25 percent payroll taxes to the Institute of Social Security Regulation. Retirement age has been set at sixty-five for men, sixty for women.[9]

By March of 1995 Chile's private pension system managed an investment fund of $23 billion—an astounding sum in a country of 14.2 million people with a GDP of $48 billion. The investment of the $23 billion breaks down this way: government bonds, 38 percent; common stock, 33 percent; mortgage securities, 13 percent; bank term deposits, 8 percent; corporate bonds, 7 percent; and non-Chilean investments, 1 percent.[10] In mid-1995, Chile's Superintendency of Pension Fund Administrators increased the limit of foreign investment allowable by AFPs to 9 percent.[11]

Since the system began operating in mid-1981, the average annual return on investment in real terms—that is, adjusted for inflation—has been 12.8 percent. It is designed to provide a pension equal to 70 percent of a worker's final salary, plus survivor's benefits. Anyone taking early retirement receives a pension worth a minimum of 50 percent of their final salary. When an AFP pensioner dies, account money becomes a part of that person's estate. Currently, six out of seven retiring workers have AFP savings that yield pensions greater than the government-subsidized 50 percent replacement rate.[12]

There are sixteen AFP companies, some affiliated with insurance companies or banks, others with labor unions or trade associations. Aetna Life and Casualty, Bankers Trust Co., CIGNA, and Spain's Banco Santander are among international partners in the various AFPs, which compete with each other for worker investment money.[13] Their performances are closely watched not only by the Chilean government, but also by workers seeking real results. Workers are free to change from one AFP to another; their pensions are totally portable.

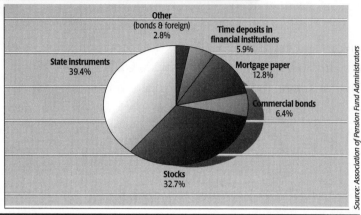

Chile Diversifies Its Private Pension Investments to Fuel Strong Returns

Other (bonds & foreign) 2.8%
Time deposits in financial institutions 5.9%
State instruments 39.4%
Mortgage paper 12.8%
Commercial bonds 6.4%
Stocks 32.7%

Source: Association of Pension Fund Administrators

Chile's pension investment portfolio as of June 1995.

Chart 23

Contributions to AFP investment accounts are tax-free, though distributions are taxed. Just as he or she might visit the bank to check on a personal savings account, a worker can go to an AFP branch, call up the individual account on a computer terminal, and see how investments are doing and what pension benefits could be expected in the year of retirement.

CHILEAN CAVEATS

Chile, with a largely homogeneous population of 14.2 million and a fast-growing economy, is not like the United States, with its 265 million people and a mature, slower-growing global economy. Moreover, Chile has a much younger population than that of the United States. Only 7 percent of Chile's population is aged sixty-five or older, compared to 13 percent in the United States.[14]

Nevertheless, there is a lesson to be learned from Chile's success. Chile's courageous reforms and growth occurred while the nation was changing from a military dictatorship to a democracy. General Pinochet, *caudillo* since 1973, was defeated in the 1989 presidential election and succeeded by Patricio Aylwin. Today Chile is negotiating to join the North American Free Trade Agreement, already belongs to the Asia-Pacific Economic Cooperation Alliance, and is exploring a treaty with the European Union.

REFORM RIPPLES: MEXICO, PERU, AND ARGENTINA

Though copper is Chile's leading export, the nation's pensions reform is fast becoming a popular export, too. Variations have been introduced in Mexico, Peru, and Argentina in the 1990s.

Mexico's reform, enacted by decree in 1991, was designed by still another University of Chicago economist, Agustin Carstens, treasurer of Banco de Mexico. Since mid-1992, employers have been required to contribute 2 percent of each worker's earnings into a private savings fund known as an SAR, which stands for *Sistema de Ahorro para el Retiro*. Workers are free to choose which SAR to go to and may also make tax-free contributions to the SAR account. The employer's contribution is in addition to the 7.5 percent it must continue to pay into the state-run Mexican Social Security Institute (IMSS) and the 5 percent it pays into a housing fund—for a total of 14.5 percent.[15]

Mexico, with ninety-four million people, is the most populous country in recent years to initiate a mandatory, supplemental retirement savings system. Also a comparatively young country, with only 4 percent of its population over sixty-five, it is projected to age fast, and its pay-as-you-go system is already in deficit.

The IMSS, patterned after the U.S. Social Security system, may eventually be replaced by the SAR system; for now, the two will operate side by side. As the government slowly increases the level of SAR contributions, to as high as 10 percent of earnings, it will cut back on the payroll contributions to the other programs.

The money from the SAR is administered by a commercial bank chosen by the worker. The bank in turn invests the funds with the Mexican Central Bank, which promises a yield of 2 percent above inflation. When the Mexican worker retires, the money in the SAR account can be taken in a lump-sum payment or can be used to purchase an annuity. Both come with tax exemptions up to certain levels. There are proposals to permit a worker to put his or her SAR account with an insurance or stock brokerage house.

The long-term prospects for reform of pensions and other programs were rocked by the 1994 peso devaluation. The financial and political crisis and subsequent U.S.-led bailout of the Mexican economy add evidence to the need for widespread and genuine reform. The transition to personal pensions continues, fine-tuned in the wake of 1994, with financial institutions as well as the government under closer scrutiny. The state-run pension system, where devaluation and inflation have ravaged retirees' benefits, was much harder hit than the personal retirement accounts.

Personal savings continue to climb: before the personal pension program commenced, there were fifteen million bank accounts in Mexico. The new system added another ten million bank accounts or other financial accounts within a year, according to Bank of Mexico estimates.[16]

Peru, where inflation has been measured in triple and quadruple digits, aims to move more quickly than Mexico to a Chilean model. It began its transition in mid-1993. Citibank Corporation, Aetna Insurance, and Holland's ING Group are among the top foreign corporations invested in Peruvian AFPs.[17]

EUROPE: TAMING THE MONSTER

Sometimes, the Social Security monster grows intractably to such proportions that it can scarcely be tamed. To propose pension reform neither slakes the beast's appetite nor trims its claws.

Italy has one of the most generous, bloated, old-age systems in the world. The nation has finally been pushed, prodded, and dragged into doing battle with its overburdened system by the indefatigable Lamberto Dini, who became prime minister in 1995 and who was the central banker and former treasury minister in the previous government headed by Silvio Berlusconi. Dini succeeded in getting legislators to approve a former anathema—a private alternative to the gluttonous state program. Amazingly, Parliament passed Dini's reform plan in July 1995, with the backing of both business and labor.

The year before, after Dini, as treasury minister, pleaded for dramatic pension cuts, labor mounted crippling strikes throughout the country. The plan was promptly dropped by Berlusconi's coalition government, which subsequently fell.

Surveying the Italian political scene then, *The Economist* published a report headlined "Dini, Fini, Miney, Mo." Several months later, it corrected: "Dini Not Yet Fini." Resurrected as prime minister, largely on the strength of his business acumen, Dini assembled a cabinet of technocrats and business executives who shared his vision. They made cutting the deficit and reforming the pension system prime objectives, including creation of a private pension program.

As in Mexico, the 1995 Italian law created a voluntary private pension system that now operates in tandem with the government-run pension system. The goal, however, is to eventually phase out Italy's state system and replace it with a private plan.[18]

Under the state program known as *tratamento fine de rap-*
porto or TFR, payroll taxes paid by the worker (8.34 percent)
and employer (21.3 percent) fund retirement pensions from the
National Social Insurance Institute.[19]

Beginning in January 1996 Italian workers can redirect 4 percentage points of the employee and employer TFR tax to the new

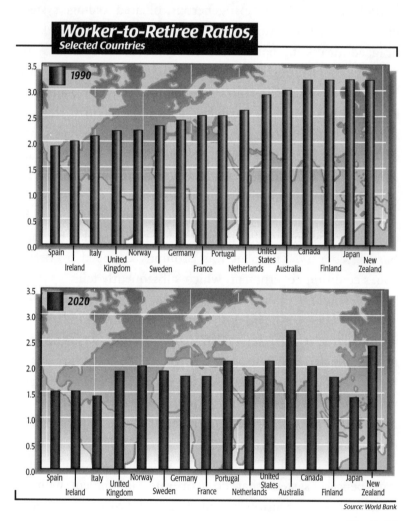

Worker-to-Retiree Ratios,
Selected Countries

Source: World Bank

Chart 24

private pension fund. Contributions are tax-free only up to 2.5 million lire ($1,500). The contribution rate to the private fund is expected to increase in the coming years.[20] The private funds will be managed by authorized banks and insurance companies.

Since the new Italian program is a defined contribution plan, as in Chile and Peru, a fund's performance influences the ultimate payback, although a minimum, inflation-adjusted return is guaranteed. After retiring, the worker can purchase an annuity or elect an annuity and a lump-sum payment.

Reformer Dini was finally *fini*. He resigned as prime minister on 11 January 1996 after realizing that he no longer had a majority in Parliament, thus ending the fifty-fourth government in postwar Italy. While his term was brief and his pension reform only a beginning step, his contribution remains significant. Against long odds, he managed to initiate reform that others can build on. Others inevitably will expand on his efforts, because they must. Contribution rates to the private funds are expected to increase in coming years, and workers can expect better returns from the private funds than the state system, which is being cut back.

ROCKING BRITAIN'S WELFARE CRADLE

Britain, the birthplace of cradle-to-grave welfare, began to rock its cumbersome cradle as early as 1978, shaking both sides of the cradle.

On 6 April of that year, social security taxes on British workers jumped from 16.5 percent to 18.5 percent, with the promise of benefit increases in retirement. At the same time, Britain began letting qualified workers opt out—or "contract out"—of a portion of the state program. Workers were permitted to redirect a portion of their payroll tax to an approved private pension plan. Those who did contract out paid less in payroll taxes and received less in government retirement benefits than those who remained with the government system.[21] But they also had the greater likelihood of a better return on investment from their private pension than the state could ever provide. By 1981 almost half of Britain's workers were enrolled in private pension plans—and the bulk of them had contracted out of a part of the state plan.[22]

Even as workers rushed into private plans, they remained plugged into a major portion of the overburdened state-run system, which other workers opted to stay with entirely. Britain's state-run pension system provides a flat-rate pension and a state earnings-related pension system (SERPS). Both plans are supported by employer–employee contributions. Men may collect benefits at age sixty-five; women, at sixty. Sixteen percent of Great Britain's population is sixty-five or older, compared to only 13 percent in the United States. It is the SERPS program that workers can contract out of in favor of private retirement plans.

By 1995 social security spending, including welfare, unemployment, and old-age pensions, consumed one-quarter of Great Britain's budget, and cost every British worker $23.70 a day.[23]

"The evidence of the lamentable performance of government in running any business—or indeed administering any service—is so overwhelming that the onus should always be on statistics to demonstrate why government should perform a particular function rather than why the private sector should not," observed Margaret Thatcher in her 1993 autobiography.[24]

Thatcher began developing her disdain of bureaucracies generally and government-run pension systems specifically as junior minister at the Ministry of Pensions in the early 1960s. "She lived on a daily diet of individual complaints and inquiries about national insurance and national assistance," notes her biographer, Hugo Young.[25]

As prime minister from 1979 to 1990, she enthusiastically preached the gospel of privatization of industry and services. Under the Thatcher government, Personal Equity Plans (PEPs) were introduced in 1986 "to encourage personal investment in shares as a way of encouraging popular capitalism,"[26] and the opportunity to contract out of the SERPS pension program was extended to more workers in 1987 and 1988.[27]

Employers, as well as workers, are encouraged to opt out of SERPS. Those employers who do contract out of SERPS must provide a private pension plan for their employees, offering at least as much in benefits as the government program does.

A pension scandal in Britain during the early 1990s rocked the reform cradle and temporarily slowed the government's privatization campaign. There were press reports of abuses by pension salesmen saddling customers with top-heavy policies to juice up commissions. A subsequent industry shakeout, leading to Parliament's tightening regulations and disclosure rules in 1995, ultimately should benefit the investor and help the government's continuing pension reform efforts under Prime Minister John Major.

Spending one-quarter of its budget on social programs has awakened England's legislators to the need for continued and radical reform of the country's welfare system. Already implemented are tax breaks for workers with individual retirement savings and annuity accounts—at banks and life insurance companies, and in mutual funds—to encourage them to save. Similar tax incentives can also be found in Canada and Switzerland.[28]

Additional impetus for pension reform likely will come from the twelve-member European Union (EU), of which Britain is a member. Article Two of the EU's Maastricht Treaty calls for "a high level of employment and social protection." The treaty also commits its signatories to lowering debt. These goals exert pressure on England, Italy, France, and the other EU nations to seek more private sector solutions to fund retirement.

DOWN UNDER, UP AND OVER

Australia's old-age and pension system, begun in 1908, is neither the oldest nor the most generous. But it is proving costly to the government—and ultimately to Australians—as the population ages. The government-run system is funded not with payroll contributions, but entirely out of general revenues. And to the traditional list of benefits, many retirees can add telephone allowances, "remote area" supplements, and rental allowances for low-income seniors.[29]

In the private sector, at least until the mid-1980s, work-related pensions in Australia were mainly a perk for the higher paid, reaching barely 40 percent of the working population—many of them government workers. But over the past dozen years, that pattern has changed dramatically as unions have demanded more pension coverage. Fully 80 percent of all workers are now covered.

Over the same years, as the life expectancy of Australians rose from seventy-eight years for women and seventy-one years for men in 1986 to eighty years for women and seventy-four years for men by 1992, demographic pressures were building for a major overhaul of Australia's public pension system.

In an effort to lighten its burden—and that of coming generations of Australian taxpayers—the government passed a sweeping pension reform bill in 1992, introducing a mandatory Superannuation Guarantee Charge (SGC) that all employers must deposit into qualified private investment funds for their workers' retirements.

Small companies currently must contribute 3 percent of a worker's earnings, while large companies must contribute 5 percent. Contribution rates for all employers will rise to 9 percent per worker by 2002.[30] So far, workers' contributions have been voluntary. But mandatory savings deductions of 1 percent will begin in 1997.[31] That could rise to 3 percent by 2002.[32] That would mean a total of 12 percent of national payrolls going into privately managed pension accounts overseen by a government-run Insurance and Superannuation Commission.

Not surprisingly, this new scheme is already leading to a vast increase in pension assets, which are projected to rise from about $170 billion (U.S.) in 1994 to more than $1 trillion by the year 2020.[33] Over time these privately invested, privately owned pension assets will substantially lower the burden of retirement costs for Australia's government—and the country's taxpayers.

In presenting the nation's 1995 budget, Australia's treasurer Ralph Willis noted that the new superannuation scheme will be "the favored means of meeting [the government's] retirement income objectives." According to the treasury, the system could lead to a net national savings increase of about 4 percent per year of GDP by the year 2000.[34] Still, it will take well into the next century for private assets to rise to the level that would allow most Australians to earn enough from their own holdings to receive only "partial" pensions from the government.

Even so, Australia's effort to "privatize" the country's retirement finance system partially is already winning favorable notices. The World Bank's 1994 report, *Averting the Old Age Crisis,* notes that "the transition in Australia consists of adding a second, 'savings' pillar to a redistributive public pillar—a move that will head off pressures that might otherwise have developed for an enlarged public pillar. Most other OECD [Organization for Economic Cooperation and Development] countries will have to go through the more painful process of separating the savings and redistributive functions and of reshaping and downsizing their public plans to avoid massive distortionary and evasionary effects as dependency rates and system costs rise."

THE KRONOR STOPS HERE

Anyone tempted to dismiss these trends as isolated and irrelevant experiments rather than responses to a fast-growing global imperative need only look to Sweden.

Long the incubator of generous social welfare policy, the Swedish model is a prime candidate for the economists' Agonizing Reappraisal Department. It is being forced to redraft its social contract with its citizens. Sweden can no longer afford the state pensions to which only a few years ago workers contributed nothing from their paychecks, while employers forked over more than 19 percent of a worker's earnings.[35]

"My country is now in the process of building a new Swedish model based on the best in the old model but avoiding its mistakes," K. G. Scherman, director–general of Sweden's National Social Insurance Board, said last year.[36]

Many of the changes, resulting from years of hearings and studies, are the patches that have been tried in the United States—pegging benefit adjustments more closely to economic growth, trimming benefits, raising the retirement age, and taxing workers. By 1995 workers were paying 1 percent of earnings to the government's universal pension program.[37] The worker contribution rate will rise several percentage points in the coming years, and the employer contribution will decline.

Most of the funds will continue to go into the government's pay-as-you-go system. What is new and promising in the reforms is the plan to put 2 percentage points of the combined worker–employee contributions into what's being called a premium reserve system—"a fully funded supplement with individual accounts," according to Scherman.[38] What is still being debated is whether the "premium reserve system" would be invested in government bonds and/or private equities. The fact that private markets are being considered at all is significant, indeed.

A booklet published in 1993 by Sweden's National Board of Health and Welfare makes an admission that bodes well for true pension reform there and worldwide. "Public sector pension systems and occupational pensions paid under agreements between employer and labor organizations together provide a high level of protection for individuals," according to *Growing Old in Sweden.* "In spite of this, there may be a need for additional private pension benefits."[39]

CHOOSING A MAKE AND MODEL

The Swedish model is fast giving way to the Chilean model. Economist Jose Pinera has gone on to become president of the International Center for Pension Reform and co-chairman of the Cato Institute's Project on Social Security Privatization. (Bill Shipman, this book's co-author, is the other co-chairman.) Pinera has lectured widely in Europe and the United States on private solutions to the global pension crisis and has consulted with the presidents of Argentina, Brazil, Colombia, Ecuador, and Brazil.

The countries that have boldly started hacking their way out of the retirement thicket can teach other nations, including the United States. They offer not so much precise examples, but rather proof that solutions mean getting out rather than plunging in deeper. There are many models throughout the world, some with particularly attractive features. As we look around the world, we are affirmed that just as other nations have started to solve their retirement funding problems, so too can the United States.

PART II

CHAPTER TEN

PATHWAY
TO A BRIGHTER
RETIREMENT FUTURE

I MAGINE THE IMPOSSIBLE. Imagine a day when America, her workers, future workers, and retirees—you and everyone in your family—no longer worry about Social Security. Retirement no longer looms like a thunderhead. Nor do Bipartisan Commissions on Entitlement or Tax Reform and Advisory Councils on Social Security issue reports of the system's imminent collapse. No more front-page horror stories about retirees facing destitution, no more baby boomer uneasiness about the debt they will inherit from a flawed Social Security system.

The alarm on Social Security has rung, and rung loud. Amazingly, the three generations once locked in combat over Social Security, and what to do about it, are now allies. When extended families—yours and ours—now gather at the holiday dinner table, the tottering Social Security system is no longer a hot topic of discussion among the generations.

Social Security is no longer the third rail of politics. America's citizens, businesses, unions, financial institutions, interest groups, and Congress have come together to resolve, finally and equitably, the system's problems.

Imagine working Americans saving at two and three times the rates of the early 1990s, investing wisely and seeing their retirement nest eggs grow. Imagine that the already retired are secure, their pensions solid. Instead of inheriting a crushing debt left by their elders, future workers find they will be more—not less—safe than their parents were when their turn to retire finally comes. At last, the opportunity of retiring with dignity is available to Americans of all ages. Meanwhile, the economy grows briskly, and the deficit is brought under control.

This scenario is neither fantasy nor delusion. It is possible, practical, and vitally necessary to America's health and welfare.

PSSA: RESCUING A FUNDAMENTAL FREEDOM

This is all possible, but only if we face up to the reality that Social Security cannot continue to work as presently constituted. Throughout the country there is a growing consensus among Americans of varying ages, economic classes, and political parties that we can no longer rely upon Social Security to provide a secure retirement for the elderly.

For if we continue with the current system, we will soon face the prospect of two workers paying taxes to support each retiree—a scenario that would create an intolerable tax burden on every American worker, a burden that would inevitably harm vulnerable retirees.

So we must have the courage to change. The question is what sort of change is most appropriate.

We do not believe that any one solution constitutes a magic bullet to solve the retirement crisis looming in our nation. That is why we are so encouraged by the many good-faith efforts under way, to come up with possible solutions to the problem. Across the nation there are political leaders, academics, think-tank scholars, and others who are hard at work exploring possible solutions to this extraordinarily complex problem.

We believe in exploring any and all options—any and all possible solutions to the problem—as long as those proposals meet the principles that have guided us throughout our work:

- ❖ The first principle is that the elderly are able to retire with financial security.
- ❖ The second principle is that younger workers should be able to keep the fruits of their labor.
- ❖ The third principle is that the economy should not be unreasonably or unnecessarily burdened by achieving the first two principles.

The plan that we have developed meets these criteria. We offer it as our contribution to the national search for a solution to the retirement problem.

Our plan is called the Personal Social Security Account (PSSA). Initially running parallel to Social Security to lighten the burden of the government system, it would ultimately replace it. This new system is based on the freedom to invest one's hard-earned income in investments tied to the growth of the economy.

We propose to rescue a fundamental American freedom—the right to control one's own economic destiny. We propose that people have the freedom to invest their FICA taxes in real financial assets—stocks, bonds, bank certificates of deposit, mutual funds, and other financial instruments that grow with a healthy economy and help make an economy grow. The stock and bond markets, in particular, have helped finance our nation's economic strength and productivity. History shows that the financial return on these instruments can meet America's retirement needs at a fraction of Social Security's cost.

Under our plan every American now in the Social Security system would be protected. Anyone in the system who wished to remain would be able to do so. That includes all retirees receiving benefits and anyone now in the workforce. **No American worker now paying into Social Security would be required to leave the system or join ours.**

Here are the highlights of our plan:

❖ Each working American would have the right to have a PSSA to be invested in stocks, bonds, and other private investments that have historically produced average compound returns of between 7 percent and 10 percent per year over many years—promising far higher returns than Social Security.

❖ Investment options would necessarily include the full range of equity funds, bond funds, and international funds. Other options would include government securities; so-called stable value funds comprising GICs, Bank Insurance Contracts (BICs), and short-term investment funds (STIFs); and cash equivalent investments such as money market funds and certificates of deposits.

❖ PSSAs will be funded by a mandatory payroll deduction—but workers choosing PSSAs would no longer have to pay the employee portion of the Social Security tax.

❖ PSSAs would start up parallel to Social Security, with all current workers free to choose the new system—and equally free to stay with Social Security.

❖ Individuals would own the assets in their PSSAs. They would have property rights.

❖ After a certain date, all new workers would be required to go into PSSAs.

❖ Social Security's phase-out would be financed by three sources: (1) a continued FICA tax on employers; (2) FICA taxes from those workers who choose to remain with Social Security; (3) new government bonds issued to reflect Social Security's existing obligations—the costs of which would be fairly spread over several generations.

❖ Current retirees' Social Security incomes would not be altered by our reform. Those choosing to switch to PSSAs would receive recognition of past Social Security taxes.

❖ All workers choosing PSSAs would be eligible to contribute to the optional PSSA-Plus (see chapter 11), up to as much as the mandatory PSSA contribution. (We will present our recommendation for the mandatory PSSA contribution rate in a later chapter, along with our reasoning behind it.) Whatever the basic PSSA rate, those choosing an additional PSSA-Plus could save an additional amount up to that rate.

❖ Only fully qualified and government licensed banks, brokerages, insurance companies, and other financial institutions would be allowed to manage PSSA and PSSA-Plus retirement investment funds.

❖ A government-appointed board of trustees would oversee the system to avoid hazards or abuses. Intense competition among institutions—on fees, service, rates of return, and so on—would be ensured, because workers would be free to transfer PSSA funds to new managers at will.

❖ Careful investment guidelines would ensure that PSSA funds are invested commensurate to a worker's age and financial needs—with a lifetime transition from more aggressive stock investing to more conservative bond or fixed-income funds.

❖ Withdrawals from PSSAs would also be restricted—stretched out in monthly installments over expected life spans after retirement age—so that they would last for the rest of one's life.

❖ Any PSSA funds remaining at death would be personal property—which could be passed on to an owner's heirs.

❖ A basic safety net for very low income retirees would continue as now.

❖ As the number of Social Security recipients declines over time, revenue from employers' FICA taxes would continue to retire the government bonds issued to finance the transition.

❖ The PSSA plan would increase U.S. savings, raise retirement benefits while reducing the payroll tax, lower the cost of investment capital, and become a matter of personal responsibility for all Americans.

We believe that anyone choosing a PSSA plan over Social Security would be far better off come retirement. To illustrate, let's take a second look at twenty-eight-year-old Brad Composite, the post-boomer we met in chapter 7. Like many of his contemporaries, this Generation Xer is a bottom liner. What's the bottom line? While he's settling in and feeling better about his job as a telephone company service rep and its prospects, he feels less and less comfortable about the payroll tax he has to pay Social Security—a program in which he and his contemporaries have little faith. If Brad could invest in stocks what he currently must pay the government in payroll taxes, by the time he retires at age sixty-seven in 2035 his portfolio will likely have accumulated $1 million. His nest egg would be enough to generate an initial retirement income of almost $88,000 a year—or $7,331 a month![1] That is 34 percent more than what Brad would get from Social Security, even assuming it could pay the benefits it is currently promising for Brad's retirement, which is unlikely.[2]

Though Brad is an actuarial composite, the estimates of stock performance are based on historic rates of return. Comparable projections for Social Security are no more than political promises, made in the face of predictions by Social Security's own trustees who admit that the system will be insolvent before Brad retires.

Brad's dilemma reflects the fundamental challenge of our future: do we rely on a failing, costly system—or on a proven market mechanism for producing and then preserving wealth? In our scenario, real investments in a growing economy provide the powerful engine that runs the PSSA plan. And you don't need to be a Wall Street master of the universe to reap the benefits.

Each worker in the PSSA plan contributes a fixed wage or salary percentage to his or her individual account, which is then invested in a fund of stocks and bonds by a financial institution the worker chooses. In the following pages, we illustrate the compounding power of retirement income that accumulates in a PSSA at various worker contribution rates.

Deposits to the PSSA would be made automatically through payroll withholding at work. While PSSA deposits for those joining the program will be mandatory to ensure steady accumulation of retirement funds, the PSSA will be just that, an invested savings account controlled by individual depositors for their exclusive retirement use. Our PSSA action plan shifts resources and control from the government back to individuals. Kids flipping burgers, CEOs driving vast enterprises, and all the workers in between will be free to plan their own retirement.

MARY AND JOHN BOOMER:
FORTY-SOMETHING AND MARRIED

Mary and John Boomer, a married couple who are both forty-one, were born in 1955, near the peak of the baby boom that will ultimately swamp Social Security. They sampled and survived the 1960s, became careerists in the 1970s, bought their three-bedroom home in the 1980s, and find themselves in the 1990s wondering about how they'll ever retire in the 2000s. After their two children leave home and the mortgage is paid, Mary and John might—*might*—be able to retire around 2021 in their mid-sixties. Or will they? Under the present arrangement, Social Security will be struggling to cough up the couple's earned retirement benefits.

No similar money bind hampers the growth of real investments in the American or global economies. Nor is it too late for Mary and John Boomer to make up for lost time in building real investments for a comfortable retirement.

But Mary and John are cautious. They wonder whether investing their precious retirement money in financial markets—stocks, bonds, and mutual funds made up of both—is safe. They wonder what will happen if the stock market crashes.

Will their money be at risk? Could tremors in the market deprive them of the funds they'll need in old age?

They ask the right questions. But the evidence is overwhelmingly on the side of long-term reliability in the financial markets. While markets fluctuate, sometimes wildly in the short run, over the long haul they have always—*always*—gone up. To analyze long-term performance of investment markets in the United States over the past seven decades is to discover that annual equity returns have usually run in double digits, while returns on bonds have risen, but with less volatility. From 1926 to 1995— through the market crash of 1929, the Great Depression, and including the massive correction in October of 1987—the stock market has offered substantial return on investment. From 1926 to 1995 large company stocks registered average annual returns of 10.5 percent, while stocks of smaller companies scored returns of 12.5 percent annually. Comparable rates from 1971 to

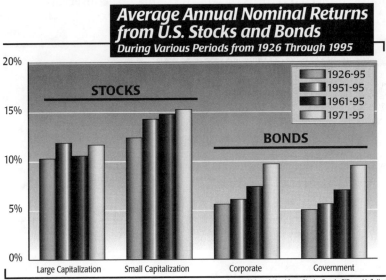

Source: Values derived from *Stocks, Bonds, Bills and Inflation* (Chicago: Ibbotson Associates, 1996)

Chart 25

1995 were 12.2 percent and 15.5 percent, respectively. Corporate bonds in the past two decades generated annual returns of 10.6 percent; government bonds, 10.4 percent.[3]

Ironically, the stock market crash of 19 October 1987 only strengthens the case for stocks. On that day the Dow Jones Industrial Average plunged an astounding 508 points, a staggering one-day decline of 22 percent. But even with that free fall, the stock market for 1987 was up 5 percent.

Impressive as returns on American stocks and bonds have been, they actually understate the investment opportunities and earnings potential for Mary and John Boomer, as well as Brad and every other American, because the U.S. market is only one, albeit the largest, of many others around the world. U.S. equities account for less than 40 percent of the total value of all equities in the world.[4] In portfolios structured to take advantage of appropriate foreign markets, which often outpace the United States, projected returns of 10 percent may be conservative.

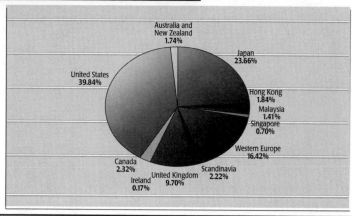

Source: Morgan Stanley Capital International On-Line Service

Chart 26

THE PSSA OPTION: PERSONAL CHOICE

By tapping into the returns in the financial markets, PSSAs offer much greater savings potential than Social Security. Many PSSA participants—particularly those who enter the program at a relatively young age—would see their retirement contributions grow into twice the aggregate amount they would otherwise receive under Social Security. Most Americans would fare considerably better under PSSAs than under Social Security.

To reiterate: no current worker would be forced to leave Social Security. No current worker would be forced to join the PSSA program. We want Americans first to understand our plan fully, assess its impact on them, and only then make the important decision whether to leave Social Security and join the PSSA program. We advocate giving the PSSA option to every person already in the labor force and enrolled in Social Security. The benefits of the PSSA will be so clear that we believe almost everyone will choose the new system. However, our plan will require all first-time entrants to the job market to enroll in PSSA so that they, too, can have the assets necessary for a secure retirement.

Employers will be key players in a successful PSSA plan, and they stand to benefit from the transition. All employers, from General Motors to the proprietor of the corner deli, must now match each worker's payroll contribution to Social Security. The obvious question is, if a worker switches to the PSSA, will the employer also switch its matching contribution?

The less-than-obvious answer is no. The employer will not make contributions to a PSSA. The PSSA is a personal, private account funded by the worker for the worker's retirement—and no one else's. Of course, one could set up a system in which employers contributed to their employees' PSSAs, even as some employers today contribute to their employees' 401(k) plans.

But the employers' portion of Social Security will still be needed to fund the obligations of the old Social Security system as it is phased out. So the employer will continue to make payments to Social Security for each worker it employs. The good news, however, is that PSSAs will be so productive that they will produce a better payoff from the employees' contributions alone than the old Social Security system produced from the combination of employers' and employees' contributions.

PAYING THE BILLS DURING PHASE-OUT

One of the principal challenges we confront in moving to a private, self-funded system is financing the transition. We have no illusions; this is an enormous challenge. Under the PSSA system, workers will be paying into their own retirement accounts—not into Social Security. Yet society still has to meet its financial obligations to both existing retirees and to future Social Security recipients. This so-called unfunded liability is measured in trillions of dollars. Some of these costs will be offset by employers' FICA taxes and by the FICA taxes of workers who elect to remain in Social Security. However, while significant, these revenues will cover only a piece of our accrued liability.

The government will have to raise additional funds to pay the balance of the bills that are coming due. One alternative is new taxes. We oppose this approach because it imposes too heavy a burden on the current generation. A second option—cuts in federal spending although meritorious in their own right—is unlikely to produce by itself the necessary savings. We believe the best financing alternative is for the government to issue long-term debt—long-maturity Treasury bonds. This option allows society to pay off Social Security's outstanding bills over several decades. We believe that no single generation should shoulder the whole transition financing. At the same time, all generations will reap the rewards of a new structurally sound retirement system—one where real money goes into real accounts that employees control.

All who join the PSSA plan will invest their own money in their own individual accounts for their own retirement. These are their assets over which they have property rights. As the number of Social Security beneficiaries begins to wind down, so, too, does the need to tax employers—ultimately eliminating their payroll tax. Since most economic research shows that the employers' portion of Social Security is for all intents and purposes a tax on workers, reducing or phasing it out should ultimately cause both an increase in wages and employment. Social Security does not crash; instead, it begins a slow, descending glide, winding down forever with the death of the last beneficiary.

While we believe that our plan could go a long way toward solving the problem, we are under no illusions. We understand that in a nation such as ours change is usually an incremental process. We do not offer our proposal with the expectation that it will, as constituted, become the law of the land.

We offer it, instead, with the sincere hope that it will further stimulate the already vigorous public debate on the retirement issue. And as this debate continues, other proposals should also be subjects of discussion. There are three plans, for example, that emerged from the administration's 1996 Advisory Council on Social Security, and we believe there are a number of attractive ideas within these plans that merit close attention.

One of the plans offered by council members, in fact, bears striking similarities to the proposal we have made. It is called the Personal Security Accounts (PSAs) plan.

This plan would create mandatory PSAs, similar in many ways to the Personal Social Security Accounts we have outlined.

Under this proposal, workers would establish an account in which 5 percent of the worker's payroll tax would be reserved exclusively for retirement.

The returns under this idea would likely be quite attractive. Assuming a 10 percent return on investment, the replacement rate for a twenty-one- and thirty-five-year-old would be 69 percent and 35 percent, respectively. Another big plus to this plan is that it would eventually lead to the Social Security system's unfunded liability falling to zero. This would be a triumphant moment for our nation.

There are other attractive aspects of this idea. The assets would be one's personal property. This plan not only recognizes the benefit of market returns but also the personal property rights of individuals' investments.

The only aspect of this plan that gives us pause is that it requires an additional 1.5 percent payroll tax. We believe that American workers are taxed too much, not too little, and that such a broad-based tax could have a dampening effect on the economy. We believe, as we have made clear, that the transition would be better funded via long-term debt. This proposal, as is the case with all three council options, would raise the retirement age, in this case to age sixty-eight for workers becoming eligible for benefits in 2017.

The second council proposal calls for requiring workers to deposit 1.6 percent of payroll, above and beyond the existing payroll tax, into individual accounts. These accounts would not be held by Social Security but as supporters of the plan put it, "they would be subject to necessary regulatory restrictions to make sure they were invested in reputable financial instruments."

Funds from these accounts would be "converted to minimum guarantee indexed annuities" at the time of retirement. When benefits from these investments are received at retirement, they would be exempt from federal income taxes.

Under this proposal, individuals would have limited choices of how their 1.6 percent of payroll would be invested. This plan would also lead to inclusion of noncovered state and local government workers in the Social Security system.

The major drawback to this proposal is that it would precipitate a significant reduction in benefits.

Over several decades the combination of reducing benefits but not taxes, while building some retirement nest egg from the mandatory savings, eventually would eliminate Social Security's unfunded liability—a big plus.

After the transition, the steady-state environment would be a 10.6 percent payroll tax, a 1.6 percent savings rate, and a replacement rate approximating 54 percent. From an investment point of view, however, this is a big negative. A 54 percent replacement rate costing 12.2 percent of payroll is substantially below market returns.

Finally, some council members offered a proposal that will surely be part of the national debate, but it is a plan that we believe would not solve the nation's looming pension crisis. It would merely put off the tough decisions for some future generation.

This Maintenance of Benefit reform plan would keep Social Security essentially as it is today. Additional funds for retirees would be raised by increasing income taxes on Social Security recipients. All Social Security benefits over already taxed employee contributions would be taxed. This idea, according to its sponsors, would eventually lead to "the complete and consistent income tax treatment of all Social Security benefits."

Another provision would require state and local government employees hired after 1997 to join the Social Security system.

Many state and local government employees are enrolled in other pension plans.

This proposal also calls for investing a portion of the OASDI trust funds in the equity markets. Over time, a total of about 37 percent of the assets in the trust fund would be invested in this way. Supporters of this plan contend that the higher returns of equity markets would enable the Social Security system to pay higher benefits or reduce taxes.

We have a fundamental disagreement with this plan in that we do not believe that the system as presently constituted is capable of serving the retirement needs of Americans, with only minor adjustments here and there.

We have a philosophical disagreement with the elements of this plan that call for reducing benefits and raising taxes, moves that would breach two of the principles that have guided us. Benefit cuts and tax hikes help Social Security's cash flow problems in the short term, yet neither addresses the flaws of pay-as-you-go financing. A change in taxes and benefits may be beneficial to the transition if fundamental reform is central. But by themselves, they cannot solve the problem.

The suggestion within this plan that some of the trust fund money be invested in equities is intriguing. We applaud the notion of moving in the direction of private investment. But there are troublesome aspects to this idea. The government would own the equity and theoretically use it as collateral to help pay its benefit liability. As a matter of law, however, benefits would be no more certain than under the present scheme of IOUs—the obligation to pay them is not determined by the collateral. Also, it should be noted that, relative to the private sector, the government has little investment experience; that, in addition to its political power, it would own the means of production, which is the definition of socialism, and investment decisions most likely would be politicized. On the plus side, Social Security's taxes would no longer be able to pay for other government spending.

In spite of our objections to this plan, we are nonetheless encouraged that inherent within it is the recognition that private investment of retirement assets is a positive step.

And that is what is so remarkable about the debate over Social Security. Not long ago the idea of private investment of Social Security funds was greeted with derision. But now it is accepted as a viable, mainstream concept.

More and more, the question is not whether to have private investment of Social Security funds, but how—and how much.

CHAPTER ELEVEN

REPLACEMENT LEVEL

I N THE TOWN of Perry, Florida, new-automobile registrations
shot up 45 percent in 1993. That was the year Procter &
Gamble sold its local pulp paper mill and separated one
thousand workers from the retirement plan—giving them large
lump-sum settlements in exchange.[1]

Those lump-sum buyouts were "a great boost to our car dealers and major appliance dealers," reported Cherry Goodman,
president of the Chamber of Commerce in Perry. A retiree
observed: "The wives are driving white Lincolns, and the guys
are driving pickups with toolboxes in the back."[2] That's nice for
the car dealers, but those white Lincolns may not shine quite so
brightly at retirement time.

A 1995 Labor Department study confirmed when workers
get windfalls, it is hard for them to resist "the urge to splurge."
Of some sixty thousand households that got lump sum payments meant to help their retirement, 30 percent spent the
money on big ticket consumer products or paid off educational,

medical, or other bills. Another 23 percent put the money into a business or house, or paid debts. Only 21 percent invested the money in an IRA. One in five persons between the ages of fifty-five and sixty-five spent *all* of their lump-sum payments.[3]

RETIREMENT: THERE WHEN YOU NEED IT FOR AS LONG AS YOU WANT

That won't happen with PSSAs, which are designed exclusively to fund retirement. The PSSA balance at retirement, which will likely top $200,000 to $300,000 for many of today's middle-aged workers and $1 million to $2 million for young workers, may be invested in annuities or continue to be invested in stocks and bonds from which one would make periodic withdrawals. The most common form of annuities are life annuities. Under a life annuity a person pays an insurance company a fixed sum—say $300,000—and in return receives a guarantee of a certain amount of money each month for life. With a $300,000 investment a life annuity would pay approximately $2,500 per month for life, assuming the annuity is purchased around age sixty-five.

The size of the PSSA balance will be determined by the contribution rate, as well as by market performance. The higher the PSSA contribution, the higher will be the PSSA accumulation. The annuity benefit, in turn, would be driven by the PSSA balance funding the annuity and the length of the annuity. The shorter the period covered by the annuity, the higher the amount of the monthly benefit. Conversely, the longer the span of the annuity, the lower the monthly benefit.

In our PSSA calculations, we focus on annuities running from retirement to age eighty. Why eighty? It is not an arbitrary number, but one chosen with care, although it is not inflexible.

Eighty is actually a few years higher than life expectancy in the United States.

The National Center for Health Statistics calculates life expectancy at birth in 1990 was 75.4 years—71.8 years for men; 78.8 years for women.[4] Social Security estimated life expectancy at birth in 1995 to be 72.2 years for men and 79.1 years for women. And, for those who reached sixty-five that year, men could expect to live another 15.3 years; women, 19.1 years.[5] Some people won't live that long, some will live beyond that age. Nevertheless, life expectancies are averages. And calculations of annuities and retirement programs, including Social Security as well as PSSAs, must take life expectancy into account.

Thus, the age of eighty is the benchmark we use in our calculations to demonstrate the potential benefits of the PSSA and to compare the plan to Social Security.

Keep in mind that PSSA participants are not locked into funding an annuity just to age eighty. They will have the freedom to choose the term of the annuity at the outset, to readjust its period once under way, or continue to invest in markets. The plan permits participants to invest in an annuity paying higher monthly benefits over a shorter period or lower benefits over a longer period. It's largely up to each person to decide how to invest the PSSA nest egg.

To illustrate, let's take the case of a hypothetical worker who retires this year at age sixty-five and who invests in an annuity initially paying $1,000 a month—to age eighty—or $12,000 a year. If the retiree instead invested the same amount in an annuity paying over a longer period, the annual benefit would be as follows: $11,400 to age eighty-one; $10,872 to age eighty-two; $10,404 to age eighty-three; $9,984 to age eighty-four; and $9,612 to age eighty-five. In the initial scenario, this retiree starts to collect $1,000 per month for fifteen years. The annuity increases by 4 percent annually. Stretching the annuity to age eighty-five, the benefits run for twenty years at 80 percent of what they would be for fifteen years. PSSAs offer flexibility. The annuity initially calculated to, say, age eighty can be "age-adjusted" later on—its assets and benefit payments can be recalculated for a shorter or longer life expectancy as conditions warrant.

Rising life expectancy is contributing to the swelling ranks of long-lived Social Security beneficiaries who ultimately will sink the pay-as-you-go system. There is no similar life-expectancy pressure on a PSSA, because its earnings are solely for the benefit of the worker who invested in it. Rising life expectancy means more time to reap the rewards of the PSSA and its annuity, which continue to earn compound interest in retirement.

THE UNDERLYING ASSUMPTIONS
OF THE PSSA PLAN

The PSSA calculations throughout this book were done for the authors by Bruce D. Schobel, a consulting actuary, who was an actuary with the Social Security Administration from 1979 to 1988. Mr. Schobel computed the PSSAs based on several different worker contribution rates, ranging from 5.3 percent—approximately what workers now pay in Old-Age and Survivors' Insurance (OASI) payroll taxes to Social Security—to 7 percent. In all cases, contributions are based on average wages beginning this year and ending with the year preceding retirement. The PSSA earns a preretirement return of 10 percent annually. The accumulated funds buy an annuity to age eighty that earns a postretirement return of 7 percent annually. The annuity benefit increases 4 percent annually, the assumed inflation rate.

In comparisons between PSSAs and Social Security benefits, the Social Security benefits were also calculated by Mr. Schobel and were based on 1995 Social Security data, and computed under present law, using average earnings starting with age twenty-one. Mr. Schobel assumes that Social Security continues to operate under present law. Social Security's normal age of retirement figures are used, which are explained in the Social Security Administration booklet *Understanding Social Security.*

HITTING THE CRUCIAL "TARGET 42" MINIMUM

How much money do I need to retire comfortably? Would a PSSA be able to supply all my needs? How much must I contribute in order to be sure of a comfortable retirement? For workers and their spouses these are crucial questions about the PSSA plan, and the answers differ for different age groups.

Younger workers joining a PSSA, for instance, will have longer to invest and build greater balances at retirement, for higher benefits when they retire. PSSA balances of between $1 million and $2 million are not unreasonable. And the higher the PSSA balance, the bigger the annuity it will fund.

Starting a PSSA early helps: a twenty-three-year-old entry-level worker, like Jennifer Median (we met her in chapter 7), could expect PSSA growth by retirement to replace 73 percent of her final year's earnings at age sixty-seven by contributing just 5.3 percent of her wages each week. If the PSSA plan required a 7 percent payroll contribution, the annuity's replacement level would jump to 96 percent.

The older a person is when switching to the PSSA program from Social Security, the lower the PSSA's replacement potential at retirement time, because there are fewer years to invest in the retirement account. However, the PSSA's design allows all

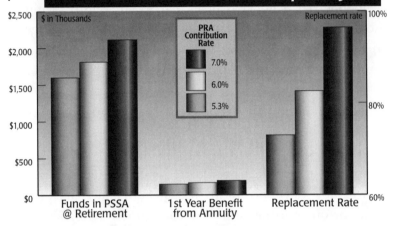

Accumulated Funds in PSSA at Retirement and Initial Annual Benefit from Annuity Provided by PRA Funds for a Worker Retiring in 2040 at Age 67. Investment Rates of Return during Working and Retirement Years are 10% and 7%, Respectively.

PRA Contribution Rate
- 7.0%
- 6.0%
- 5.3%

Funds in PSSA @ Retirement   1st Year Benefit from Annuity   Replacement Rate

Assumptions: Worker, age 23 in 1996, earns national average wages in every year. PSSA contributions start in 1996. Annuity benefits are assumed to continue from retirement to age 80 (approximate life expectancy) and increase 4% annually (assumed inflation rate).

Source: Bruce Schobel

Chart 27

workers switching from Social Security to a PSSA to achieve at least a 42 percent replacement level of their last year's earnings at normal retirement age, perhaps much more. Reaching a point where private investment provides a retiree with retirement income which equals 42 percent of one's last year's working wage is what we call "Target 42." This target is not randomly chosen: 42 percent is the replacement rate that Social Security pays at normal retirement age *now* to a worker with lifetime average earnings. And though some politicians may claim it will still be paying 42 percent of the final work year's wages twenty years from now, the reality, as we showed in Part I of this book, is that there is no way the current system can sustain such a payout. To attempt to do so would require a tax increase that could collapse the economy, even if the voters accepted it, which they almost certainly would not.

Of course, middle-aged and older workers could not accumulate enough in the PSSA before retirement to meet Target 42 from the PSSA alone. Nor should they have to. They have paid into Social Security for decades and deserve its return. So under the PSSA system they would still receive Social Security payments. Thus while they are too far along in their careers for their PSSAs to fund all their retirement benefits, they would not lose ground. Our PSSA plan would supplement the accounts of these workers. Our plan will add to their accounts an amount sufficient to get them to Target 42. For example, let's say a worker's PSSA annuity provided him with $400 per month and his Target 42 was a total of $500 per month. In that case, the government would pay the additional $100.

John Boomer, forty-one, would be an ideal candidate for this option. If John joins a PSSA in 1996 and contributes 5.3 percent of his paycheck for the rest of his career, he accumulates more than $200,000 by his retirement in 2021. That buys an annuity generating $18,000 a year, or just over half of what he will need to hit Target 42.[6] The rest of what he needs would come from a partial payment of the Social Security benefits that his FICA payments earned earlier in his career. From his FICA contributions, starting with his first job at age twenty-one and stopping at the end of 1995, Mr. Boomer would have enough Social Security–covered earnings to receive a yearly retirement benefit starting at $22,764. Under the PSSA plan, he would receive two-thirds of $22,764—but only two-thirds, since that is all he needs to reach Target 42.[7]

The very fact that middle-aged workers, such as John Boomer and his wife Mary, would still be able to collect substantial

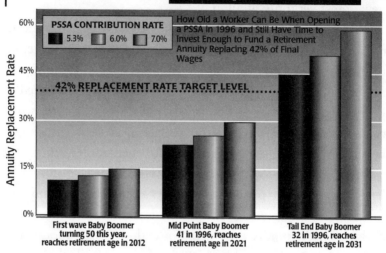

Assumptions: Workers earn national average wages in every year. Oldest and mid-point boomers retire at age 66, youngest boomer at age 67. Contributions to PSSA begin in 1996. Annuity benefits are assumed to continue to age 80 (approximate life expectancy) and increase 4% annually (assumed inflation rate).

Source: Bruce Schobel

Chart 28

benefits from Social Security even as they benefited from their PSSAs should attract many workers of their age bracket into the new system.

No such inducements are needed for younger workers. Even a worker in his early or mid-thirties can realize enough growth in a PSSA to reach Target 42. For workers that young, their PSSAs would be able to supplant Social Security totally.

DOUBLING THE PSSA ADVANTAGE
WITH PSSA-PLUS

All workers joining the PSSA plan, at whatever age, could increase their contribution level—and thus their balance and annuity at retirement time. As we envision the system, whatever their rate of the pretax mandatory contribution, workers could make substantially more—in some cases double—with what we call PSSA-Plus.

PSSA-Plus is a bonus, a supplement to income generated by the PSSA alone or by the PSSA/Social Security combination. And the great thing about PSSA-Plus is that it would not reduce your Social Security benefits if you were one of the older workers on a combined PSSA–Social Security plan. Your Social Security benefit would be fixed at the amount you would need to reach Target 42 in combination with the basic PSSA-funded annuity. PSSA-Plus earnings would not be considered in that calculation. So, if you paid in more to PSSA-Plus, you collect and keep more at retirement. You would receive the combination of PSSA and Social Security that brings you to Target 42, and on top of that you would receive whatever accrued in the PSSA-Plus plan.

CHECKING THE REGISTER: KEEPING TABS ON PSSAS

To keeps tabs on his or her PSSA, each worker joining the plan will be given a numbered PSSA monitored by regular account statements. Thanks to computers, at any time of day or night, workers will be able to check on their accounts, which will be their own personal property. Workers will be able to verify contributions made, interest earned, and current balances, and will be able to estimate "what if" scenarios. They will be able to calculate their PSSAs' likely balance at retirement and their annual benefits based on different contributions and annuity projections. It will be as simple as accessing an account on a home computer or on a customer terminal at a bank!

America's banks, brokerage houses, registered investment advisors, and mutual fund and insurance companies will be competing aggressively to manage collective trillions of PSSA dollars. Since the American financial industry is already well established, extensive, competitive, and regulated, no new breed of government-controlled PSSA agency will be needed. Current law provides ample safeguards for retirement funds. Only major institutions such as banks, brokerage houses, registered investment advisors, and mutual fund and insurance companies will be permitted to handle the retirement funds.

A government-approved board of trustees, however, will set PSSA investing guidelines to establish reasonable tradeoffs of risk and return, avoiding unnecessary hazards. But the government would not, should not, and could not guarantee returns. Government guarantees encourage riskier investments because Uncle Sam (the American taxpayer) limits the downside. For the system as a whole this does not reduce risk; it merely shifts it from the worker to the taxpayer.

The PSSA program will include a safety net: the existing Supplemental Security Income program, or SSI, funded out of the general budget, just as it is now. SSI would be available to those qualifying low-income PSSA participants whose total retirement benefits fall short of a certain adequate minimum income. This protection would apply primarily—if not entirely—to future workers, who during their careers had for whatever reason woefully underperforming PSSAs. They would receive SSI and whatever they had accumulated in the PSSA. In 1996 the maximum monthly SSI benefits are $470 for an individual and $705 for a couple.[8] SSI would rarely be needed by current workers switching to a PSSA, because they would have the option of drawing from earned Social Security benefits to supplement their PSSAs to reach Target 42.

RETIREMENT: THERE WHEN YOU WANT IT

PSSAs significantly expand a worker's choices and options.

Under Social Security, a worker can currently take early retirement at age sixty-two and collect reduced benefits, or retire at sixty-five with full benefits. (Under laws enacted in 1983, the retirement age will rise to sixty-six for workers reaching that age in 2009 and to sixty-seven for workers reaching that age in 2027.)[9]

With PSSAs, workers basically can retire when they choose, for unlike Social Security, which is age specific, PSSAs are replacement rate determined. To retire early, however, a worker must have PSSA benefits that reach Target 42 in the last year of work. PSSAs do not penalize a retiree for outside income or part-time work after retirement as does Social Security. PSSA workers are encouraged to set their own retirement course.

While PSSAs may not be ideal for today's older Americans, we believe the program far outperforms Social Security for most of the 142 million active workers now contributing payroll taxes to support current retirees—a ratio of 3.3 workers for each beneficiary.[10] Since that ratio will fall to 2.9 workers by 2010 when the baby boomers begin retiring and to two-to-one by 2030 as today's twenty-somethings start retiring, PSSAs are most definitely the right plan for them and for all future workers.

In fact, the more who leave Social Security, the lighter the burden and the sooner the system can be decommissioned.

PSSA: A TRIPLE-WIN PROPOSAL

The PSSA plan is a triple-win proposal. It is a win for workers, a win for retirees, and a win for America. The retirement future of today's young people, long in doubt, will be secure. They will have the time to invest and replace much more than 42 percent of wages and with no government help. Present retirees will not lose any benefits—a cardinal stipulation of the PSSA plan. Soon-to-retire workers can join PSSAs and not have benefits drop below the 42 percent level.

But the biggest win may come from the PSSAs' liberating effects on the U.S. economy. Almost 20 percent of our national budget goes to Social Security. To diminish and eventually eliminate that enormous expense will release the brakes on a powerful economy and create conditions for capital markets to surge. And generations not yet born will inherit a brighter future in an America where people have renewed freedom to invest for their own retirement futures.

CHAPTER TWELVE

Everything You Always Wanted to Know About the PSSA Plan

C HANGE IS OFTEN difficult because it can be confusing. That may be especially true of financial change. The prospect of change in matters involving the economic security and well being of our families can be daunting. Clearly, the PSSA plan would involve dramatic change in the way we fund retirement in the United States.

When we discuss the idea with people, we find they have many questions. And it is through the process of that discussion—through those questions and answers—that we find people's concerns being allayed.

So we're devoting some time here to answering questions that inevitably and legitimately come to mind when change of the magnitude we're discussing is proposed.

PSSAs seem like drastic reform—why not just fix Social Security?

Social Security's problems grow out of demographic shifts that cannot be fixed simply by cutting benefits or raising taxes.

Remember that Social Security is a pay-as-you-go system. This means that today's workers pay for today's retirees; similarly, benefits for tomorrow's retirees will be paid by tomorrow's workers. Thus the success of this and other pay-as-you-go systems depends largely on the ratio of workers paying into the system to retirees drawing benefits out of the system.

The problem in the United States—and in many other countries throughout the world—is that an aging population has caused this ratio to fall precipitously. In 1950 sixteen workers paid into Social Security for every beneficiary. Today that ratio has fallen to three-to-one. The ratio will drop to two-to-one early in the next century.

When many workers are supporting each beneficiary, pay-as-you-go systems can actually generate large surpluses. In fact, our Social Security system has generated considerable positive cash flow surpluses at various times in its history. However, when the ratio falls, pay-as-you-go systems come under stress. This is the situation in which we now find ourselves. Left unchanged, the system's current positive cash flows become deficits in 2013, and the system will go bankrupt around 2030. A self-funded system that engages private investment is the only lasting solution.

How does the PSSA plan deal with Social Security's demographic flaw?

It doesn't, because it doesn't have to. The PSSA system is not pay-as-you-go. The "P" in PSSA means what it says: a *personal* account that is entirely yours and stays with you wherever your work takes you. Unlike today, your payroll withholding will actually be a savings—invested by an authorized financial institution in a diversified portfolio of stocks and bonds for *your* retirement, nobody else's. Your benefits will be ensured from the nest egg that you built during your working years.

What kind of growth are we talking about?

Long-term annual returns have been 10 percent or more in equities annually. A twenty-three-year-old with average wages who opens a PSSA this year and contributes 5.3 percent of that wage to a PSSA instead of Social Security would likely have assets of $1.6 million by retirement at age sixty-seven, assuming no gaps in employment. Invested in an annuity to age eighty, that would replace 73 percent of wages in the final year of work. If the worker contributes 7 percent to a PSSA, compound earnings by retirement could total as much as $2.1 million, funding an annuity replacing 96 percent of the final work year's salary. Even if we assume market returns of 7 percent annually—far below historical performance—this same person would accumulate $1 million by age sixty-seven, or 45.5 percent replacement rate, by contributing 7 percent of his or her salary to PSSA. Social

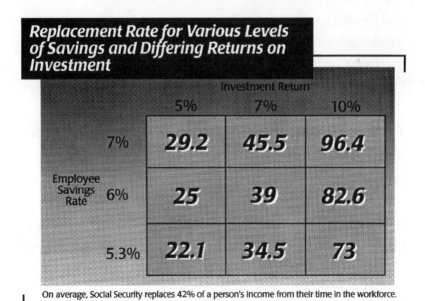

Replacement Rate for Various Levels of Savings and Differing Returns on Investment

		Investment Return		
		5%	7%	10%
	7%	29.2	45.5	96.4
Employee Savings Rate	6%	25	39	82.6
	5.3%	22.1	34.5	73

On average, Social Security replaces 42% of a person's income from their time in the workforce.

Chart 29

Security provides 42 percent replacement, but will not be able to continue even at that low level.[1]

Ten percent annual growth? Isn't that unrealistic?

Not at all. Between 1926 and 1995 the average annual nominal return was 10.5 percent for large capitalization stocks, 12.5 percent for stocks of smaller companies.[2] These rates are for U.S. markets. PSSA funds will be invested worldwide, where many markets exceed U.S. growth rates. As the accompanying matrix demonstrates, people getting a 10 percent return on investment are able to replace a very substantial amount of last year's wage. A person saving 6 percent of his or her income and who earns a 10 percent return on investment would at retirement receive 82.6 percent of his or her last year's wage.

What if my rate of return is less than 10 percent?

Replacement rates are still fairly substantial. For example, a person who saves 6 percent of their income and gets a return on investment of 7 percent would still achieve a replacement rate of 39 percent.

If Social Security is in such bad shape, why does the PSSA plan keep it running for several decades?

With thirty-eight million retirees already drawing benefits, Social Security cannot be shut down overnight. Millions more are close to retirement—too late to earn an adequate PSSA balance. They've been counting on Social Security benefits; they should get them. Young people's PSSAs will have time to grow to Target 42—the PSSA plan's target of replacing 42 percent of a worker's earnings in the year before retirement—and very likely much more. Those in midcareer or beyond will be encouraged to switch to a PSSA by making up any Target 42 shortfall with their FICA-earned benefits. For these reasons, Social Security must continue while the transition takes place.

How much can those in midcareer get by retirement?

Workers who switch to a PSSA will get whatever accrues in the PSSA, regardless of age. How much does accrue will be driven not only by market performance but also by the PSSA contribution rate adopted. We've just seen the results that contribution rates of 5.3 percent and 7 percent deliver. (In just a few pages, we will present our recommended rate and the reasoning behind it.) If a PSSA's value has not reached Target 42, only what's needed to close the gap comes from Social Security benefits earned before joining the PSSA. At the various rates we considered, workers in the midthirties and younger won't need any earned makeup benefits.

Is there any way to increase the PSSA benefit?

Yes, the PSSA plan will offer all participants the option of increasing their payroll contribution rate through PSSA-Plus. Taking full advantage of PSSA-Plus could double the PSSA annuity. PSSA-Plus earnings will not affect the amount of FICA-earned benefits later PSSA-switchers might need.

If people leave Social Security to join a PSSA, who will pay for the benefits going to today's retirees and workers who stay with Social Security?

Benefits will be financed by employee and employer FICA taxes of those who stay with Social Security, employer taxes of those who choose PSSAs, and the issuance of government bonds.

Won't the transition balloon Social Security's deficit?

The answer is yes and no. It is true that as more and more workers pay into their own PSSAs and not into Social Security, there will be less money to meet Social Security's accrued obligations. This is why we propose issuing long-term government bonds to help finance this transition.

Left unchanged, Social Security moves into so-called negative cash-flow—more money going out than coming in—beginning in 2012. As more and more of the baby boomers retire, these cash-flow deficits will grow increasingly worse, until the system ultimately collapses in 2029. An immediate switch into PSSAs will generate more immediate deficits, but will generate subsequent surpluses beginning in 2042, as the number of Social Security beneficiaries rapidly dwindles. These cash-flow surpluses would be used to pay off the bonds that were previously issued.

Who is eligible to join a PSSA?

Any worker. The choice to join a PSSA or stay with Social Security will be up to each worker. Those joining a PSSA would begin making a mandatory contribution into their accounts. Nonswitchers would continue paying the prevailing rate to Social Security. After a certain date, new workers would join a PSSA; Social Security would not accept new entrants.

If PSSAs are so superior to Social Security and this is all about freedom, why the mandatory savings?

Society will not allow people to be destitute. If the system were voluntary, the welfare of the nonsavers would be borne by the savers—giving the former a free ride and thereby reducing the benefits of the latter. This is precluded by mandatory savings.

Suppose I want to leave my PSSA? Or change my mind about Social Security?

Initially, you will be given the options of staying with Social Security or joining the PSSA plan. The logic of numbers should guide your decision. Should you choose Social Security, you may later move to a PSSA. Once in the PSSA plan, however, the decision is final. You will still have a variety of investment choices and final say on the PSSA's management.

What if I need the PSSA money sooner, say, to pay my children's college tuition or to pay off medical bills or a mortgage?

The PSSA funds will be exclusively for retirement. Other consumption can be met with PSSA-Plus and other savings.

Doesn't the PSSA plan ask a bit much of workers—like becoming instant investment rocket scientists?

No. Workers will have the right to choose which firm will manage their PSSA assets. Workers can decide to take an active or passive role in the actual investment decision. PSSA investments will be in a diversified portfolio of stocks, bonds, certificates of deposit, mutual funds, or similar instruments. The program will require that investors spread their risk within government guidelines. A competent professional fund manager diversifies such portfolios so that his or her investors are investing, in effect, in the American or world economy, not just a few companies. The rules governing PSSAs will require diversification. One should expect a lively and diverse educational and marketing campaign mounted by employers, unions, financial institutions, and interest groups. Each step of the way, the worker will have the resources and counsel of the managing financial institution. Computerized account monitoring will allow PSSA investors to track account performance, market conditions, historical data, and economic forecasts to make better informed decisions.

Will I be able to change PSSA managers?

Absolutely. Workers will be able to move PSSA accounts to whichever approved financial institution they wish, and the expected brisk competition to manage PSSAs will foster constantly improving services.

Who will watch the money managers and financial advisors?

A blue-ribbon PSSA panel of financial experts with oversight power would be set up by Congress, somewhat like the Securities and Exchange Commission, which watches the U.S. stock markets. The panel would set investment guidelines to coordinate standards ensuring equity and fairness and to protect workers from overly risky investments. It would also screen and certify that any bank, brokerage house, registered investment advisor, or insurance or mutual fund company wanting to handle PSSAs is financially sound, capable, prudent, and ethical. We fully expect the panel, government, news media, and financial advisors to be watching closely as PSSAs evolve and to spot any excess or room for improvement. There should be no shortage of oversight.

What will happen to the 10 percent annual growth on investment if the market declines, as it will sooner or later?

Yes, markets do fluctuate. But recovery has always followed downturn, especially for long-haul investors. The 10 percent growth referred to above includes both the Great Depression and Black Monday, 19 October 1987. The early 1990s have given us record bull markets; logic tells us a bear will wake up sometime. However, we have seen that even at much lower market returns, PSSAs will offer higher accumulated savings and replacement rates than Social Security. Investments can be diversified to reduce volatility and the probability of loss.

So there's no guaranteed PSSA rate of return? What will happen if my PSSA performs poorly?

PSSAs won't guarantee returns—but neither can Social Security. Social Security benefits have declined relative to taxes because of the demographic issue we have discussed. In the PSSA plan, demographics will not have this effect. Even if a worker were to receive a 7 percent return from equities—which is far below the historical average—the replacement rate would be above Target 42. However, if for some reason the replacement rate from the worker's PSSA fell below Target 42, the government would make up the difference.

Why would the PSSA be used to fund an annuity only to age eighty? I come from a family of long-lived people. What happens if I live longer than eighty?

Age eighty is an approximate life expectancy, based on Social Security and National Center for Health Statistics data. The *1995 Annual Report of the Board of Trustees* of Social Security estimates life expectancy at birth in 1995, for example, to be 72.2 years for males and 79.1 years for women.[3] PSSA earnings are intended to fund annuities, which we calculated to age eighty to illustrate the plan and to compare it to Social Security.

Since life expectancy is an average, clearly some people won't live nearly that long, while others will live beyond that point.

Keep in mind that PSSA participants will not be locked into funding an annuity only to age eighty. The plan will permit participants to invest in an annuity paying higher monthly benefits over a shorter period or lower benefits over a longer period. It largely will be up to each person to decide how to invest their PSSA nest egg.

A person retiring at sixty-seven and investing their PSSA earnings in an annuity to age eighty-five would be scheduled to receive monthly benefits for eighteen years. The benefit would be 77 percent of the amount that would be paid over thirteen years by an annuity to age eighty. PSSAs offer the flexibility. An annuity initially calculated to, say, age eighty can be "age-adjusted" later on—its assets and benefit payments can be recalculated for a shorter or longer life expectancy as conditions warrant.

What will be the spin-off benefits of PSSAs?

Weekly PSSA contributions will add up each year to billions and then trillions of invested dollars. Not only will that growing investment pool ultimately secure your retirement, but your savings will also significantly expand the nation's capital supply, thus encouraging business expansion, creating jobs, and fostering growth.

What's the next step? How close are we to having a PSSA plan?

The PSSA plan, at least in the United States, is still an idea, but one that has serious support because it fundamentally makes sense. The idea and our specific notions for implementing PSSAs need to be examined, questioned, and debated.

CHAPTER THIRTEEN

THE $7.5 TRILLION QUESTION

D OING NOTHING AND staying with Social Security will cost Americans $7,500,000,000,000.00. Simply, startlingly, that is the system's *unfunded* retirement liability as of right now.[1]

If your eyes glaze at that many zeroes, they add up to $7.5 *trillion*. Seven and one-half trillion dollars! That's how much more the nation will owe its pensioners than the system can collect under current plans. That shocking, little-known sum is the debt legacy facing our children and grandchildren. That numbing mortgage on their future also slams the brakes on our economy and job creation today. To paraphrase the late Illinois Republican Everett Dirksen: "A trillion here, a trillion there, and pretty soon you're talking about real money." Back in the 1950s Senator Dirksen used the word *billions* of dollars.

Now we tote up the debt in *trillions*—that is, thousands of billions. That $7.5 trillion is the difference between projected taxes the government hopes to collect from people currently enrolled and the total retirement benefits Social Security promised to pay only those people now retired or enrolled. In plain English, that's how much more Social Security must pay out in Old-Age and Survivors Insurance (OASI) benefits to today's pensioners and tomorrow's retirees than Social Security expects from future payroll taxes. Some dismiss the $7.5 trillion as a meaningless accounting figure or actuarial factoid—because it ignores the payroll taxes of today's children and the as-yet-unborn workers and their future employers. But the $7.5 trillion liability does not include what the system would eventually owe children and as-yet-unborn workers in benefits earned. At some point the pyramid scheme collapses.

That $7.5 trillion figure, though usually disguised in a blizzard of federal numbers, is calculated by the Social Security Administration itself. By law, the agency must produce a tally for the summary report titled *Statement of Liabilities and Other*

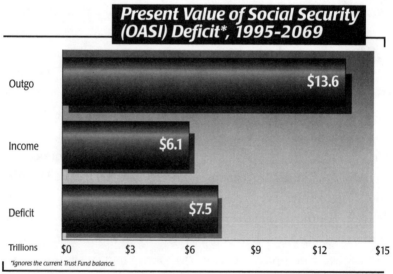

Present Value of Social Security (OASI) Deficit*, 1995-2069

Outgo	$13.6
Income	$6.1
Deficit	$7.5

Trillions $0 $3 $6 $9 $12 $15

Ignores the current Trust Fund balance.

Source: Social Security Administration

Chart 30

Financial Commitments of the United States Government, which the U.S. Treasury Department issues annually outlining the entire government's outstanding obligations.

Another calculation done by Social Security, which does include taxes to be paid and benefits earned by future workers, projects a lower but still disquieting deficit. The present value deficit—the differences between the retirement program's income and outgo between 1995 and 2069—is $2.7 trillion.[2] That tidy sum is the amount of money that Social Security needs on hand in order to meet its future obligations. While still a staggering amount, the overall deficit calculation is lower than the unfunded liability because of the tax revenue expected from generations of future workers who would not have many years in which to draw benefits in this seventy-five-year valuation period. But Bruce Schobel, a former Social Security actuary, cautions: "At the end of seventy-five years, of course, you'd fall off a cliff."[3] Social Security does not publish projections beyond seventy-five years. If it did, the grim statistics would get grimmer still.

NO OSTRICH DEFENSE: FACING THE CRUNCH

To stick our heads in the sand of quick fixes, fuzzy numbers, and pat assurances will not make this threat to our national welfare disappear. Our best hope is to enact a PSSA program.

Not only will PSSAs protect and enhance retirement; the plan will also finally gain control over Social Security's runaway liability and deficit, and thus finally shut down the broken system.

If everyone eligible joined a PSSA plan, including those on a combined PSSA–Social Security plan, Social Security's projected $2.7 trillion deficit could be reduced by a trillion dollars or more. It could even be turned into a surplus.

To illustrate the impact of small adjustments under the PSSA plan, raising the employer's rate to just 6 percent while keeping the worker's rate at 5.3 percent would trim the present value deficit to $2.1 trillion. Putting both rates at 6 percent would reduce it to $1.7 trillion. Contribution rates of 7 percent would turn the $2.7 trillion deficit into a surplus of $200 billion.[4] These reductions in the Social Security deficit are not just the result of tax increases. If that were the case we could fix the current system with a modest tax increase. Yet even the Social Security trustees admit that is impossible. To "save" the current system, payroll taxes would have to nearly double.

No, the reason PSSAs can solve the problem is that PSSA investments are real investments, producing real returns. As we wean workers away from deficit-financed Social Security to investment-financed PSSAs, the Social Security deficit disappears.

No accounting tricks are involved here; quite the contrary. A now-hidden debt, which politicians and Social Security administrators have ignored or window-dressed, will be visibly acknowledged—and paid over many decades. And unlike today, we can be sure it will be paid because the actual amount owed will be reduced as qualifying older workers who join the PSSA plan will draw less from deficit-financed Social Security benefits, and because no future debts will mount up since all future workers will be 100 percent PSSA funded.

The choice comes down to this: stick with the current plan, and our already monstrous Social Security debt will continue to grow—so large that at some point the government will be forced to officially repudiate the debt.

However, if we implement the PSSA plan that we lay out in this book, then our nation will face substantial, albeit manageable, deficits in the next four decades or so and enormous surpluses later on. Sometime around the end of the twenty-first century, Social Security will close forever as the last person receiving benefits dies. Decades before, around the early 2040s, the system will have actually begun to produce annual cash-flow surpluses, as a result of the rapidly shrinking number of beneficiaries.[5]

Implementing a successful PSSA program and realizing its benefits will take decades, of course. During the transition, the PSSA program will cause Social Security's annual cash-flow deficits to balloon immediately, instead of in 2013 as now forecast, and continue for several decades. But more important is that the sum of all the deficits under the PSSA plan will be much less than the sum of all the deficits under Social Security—trillions of dollars less.

How much the annual deficit grows, when it turns downward, and when it turns to a surplus depends on what PSSA contribution rates are adopted. A PSSA worker/employer contribution rate of 5.3 percent each would increase Social Security's annual cash-flow deficit by $500 billion in the year 2033, pushing it to $1.5 trillion total. But the deficit would begin shrinking a few years later and turn into a surplus by 2046. At 6 percent rates, the increase would be less than half as much. That combination would raise the system's projected annual cash-flow deficit by roughly $200 billion throughout the 2020s and several years thereafter. The deficit would peak, however, at $1.2 trillion total in 2033, begin to shrink, then turn into a surplus by 2043.[6]

Keep in mind that the annual cash-flow deficit—or surplus—is the balance between the outgo of earned benefits to be paid against the income of expected payroll taxes in a given year. The present value deficit discussed earlier in the chapter is a related but different calculation—money needed today to meet future obligations or the excess of outgo over income during a specific period of time.

DEFICIT FEVER: CAN WE TAKE THE HEAT?

With worker/employer rates set at 7 percent each, the annual cash-flow deficit would peak in 2033 at $800 billion total, then plunge, becoming a surplus in 2041. Higher rates would cap the deficit's growth as well as drive it down into surplus sooner. But those same, optimal PSSA savings rates—7 percent for workers and employers—would cause Social Security's annual deficits to be $100 billion to $150 billion higher than they otherwise would be between 1996 and 2017.[7]

While we believe that, given the opportunity, the vast majority of workers would join the PSSA plan, there is no way of knowing the exact proportion. To compare it against the existing Social Security system, we asked Bruce Schobel, our actuary, to don rose-colored glasses and assume that everyone eligible enrolls in a PSSA.

Since the PSSA plan gives people the freedom to say no, the actual results will fall somewhere between an unchanged Social Security and our total-enrollment scenario. Using Mr. Schobel's model, we can estimate the reduction in the deficit resulting from lower participation in the PSSA plan. For example, at a 6 percent contribution rate, if 75 percent of eligible workers join a PSSA, we would cut the present value deficit by roughly $750 billion, as opposed to the $1 trillion savings if everyone joins. At 50 percent participation, the present value deficit would drop by $500 billion. Similarly, if only a third of eligible workers join a PSSA, the deficit would be reduced by about $300 billion. Under all PSSA scenarios, once Social Security's annual cash-flow deficit is eliminated, a surplus would rapidly build that ultimately could be measured in the trillions. By contrast, without the PSSA plan, Social Security's annual deficits would continue to grow out of control year by year, decade by decade.

Under the PSSA plan, deficits would grow largest during the early and intermediate transition because workers opening PSSAs would suddenly stop paying taxes into Social Security. If everyone eligible switched to a PSSA, Social Security's tax revenue might drop by almost half, the other half being made up by employers continuing to pay into the system.

"AHA!" EXCLAIMS OUR WEARY TAXPAYER

No doubt, projections of PSSAs actually swelling annual cash-flow deficits for decades have struck a nerve in most taxpayers. We suspect many are saying: "Aha! There's the catch! Count me out!" Weary 1040 filers want to see deficits shrink, not balloon, and they want results in their wallets.

Consequently, increasing Social Security's short-term and intermediate deficits, even though it reduces the cash-flow deficit over time, is not something we propose in a cavalier manner. But we cannot in good conscience hide or minimize it.

We have crunched numbers into dust to find alternatives. But if we are to switch to the PSSA plan and still honor Social Security's obligations, there is no practical way to avoid a temporarily bigger cash-flow deficit. The traditional, more face-saving patches—tax increases, benefit cuts, means-testing, hiking retirement ages—may temporarily delay a deficit increase. But if we stick with the old solutions, America's retirement system will be drowned in debt and washed away in the deluge. Bold action now will make us stronger and more secure as a nation and an economy.

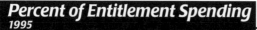

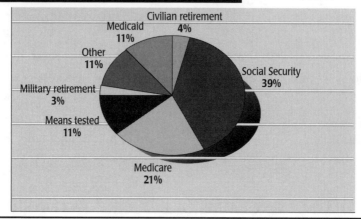

Source: Congressional Budget Office

Chart 31

Moreover, unlike the open-ended, constantly growing deficits of the current system, the initial increased deficit caused by switching to the PSSA plan will come to an end at a definite point as the old system is phased out and disappears.

FUNDING THE DEFICIT

We propose financing the temporary shortfall with government bonds—long-term debt. The PSSA approach will result in an overall decrease in the unfunded liability. Under the present system we are projected to go into deficit in 2013 and never come out of it. Under the PSSA plan we go into deficit sooner but it is temporary; we then are able to pay it off. In the near term there would be less revenue received than benefits paid. But as the finite cohort of Social Security beneficiaries dies, government benefit payments would steadily decline, ultimately falling to zero. The employers' tax on those who chose the private system would continue to pay off the debt incurred to finance the transition. In the long run no government benefits would be paid to this group because Target 42 is achieved from the PSSA alone.

Business people of all walks—from CEOs to small shop owners—may balk at having to pay taxes to support others' retirement. It is neither the intent nor the result of the PSSA plan to punish business. As advocates of free markets and deregulation, we seek to nurture business growth. We submit that employers will not lose in the PSSA transition but will benefit—just as surely as will their workers, their families, and their own retirement plans.

Also, employers will reap a direct benefit from vast investment capital pools created as trillions of PSSA dollars accumulate in the capital markets. Employers needing loans and equity financing will find trillions of dollars seeking investment opportunities.

And, finally, after the government bonds are redeemed, the employer tax would be *eliminated*. Businesses will grow, be more productive, prosper. New jobs will be created. As individual Americans finally put their financial houses in order, so too will the nation.

CHAPTER FOURTEEN

NEW SPIRIT OF '76

A NEW SPIRIT OF '76 is reborn, or can be, in the PSSA plan. Seven and six—76—are the preferred mandatory rates we recommend for the PSSA plan. The Spirit of '76 is an appropriate way to remember and promote those crucial numbers, because the PSSA plan epitomizes liberating American citizens from economic tyranny and increasing their financial independence.

Under the best scenario for everyone involved, workers joining or switching to PSSAs pay a mandatory 7 percent of wages, up to the Social Security wage limit ($62,700 in 1996) to their IRAs. All employers pay 6 percent of their workers' wages to the same $62,700 limit to Social Security.[1] Workers staying for whatever reason in Social Security pay the system's rate, presently about 10.6 percent, inclusive of the employer's tax.[2]

We chose this particular combination of rates over all the others for financial, economic, and political reasons that add up to this: 7 percent on workers enrolling in a PSSA and 6 percent on all employers best creates the desired financial benefits. Instead of a deficit exploding uncontrollably as workers leave Social Security, the resulting immediate short-term deficit increase will be moderate and manageable, and will then become a surplus. No undue strain will wrack the economy during transition. To the contrary, as we switch from a tax of 5.3 percent to a savings of 7 percent, the economy will pick up speed. The rising tide of capital will buoy businesses seeking money to expand and modernize. And America's personal savings rate is likely to increase.

THE WINNING COMBINATION

We considered several different combinations of rates for employees and employers, including one plan that sticks to the current Social Security rate of 5.3 percent. But we found that 7 percent and 6 percent are very workable and attractive. We believe they are saleable to America's workers, retirees, employers, and Congress because the rates are realistic.

The PSSA plan of 7 percent and 6 percent is simple and eminently fair. For a young worker, the 7 percent investment will replace almost all of his or her last working year's income—more than double what would come from Social Security.[3]

When Franklin Roosevelt proposed Social Security in the midst of the Depression, he lamented the "hazards and vicissitudes of life." Intended as a bulwark "against poverty-ridden old age,"[4] Social Security was built in a crisis atmosphere full of fear and pessimism. Six decades later, the PSSA plan has the power to turn today's pessimism into a hope-filled reality, creating a strong sense of common purpose—the Spirit of '76. The key to liberating people from a fearful future and creating true growth opportunities lies not in forging more government, but less.

TO THE POWER OF SEVEN

How would that promise actually play out?

The worker's mandatory payroll savings would rise by 1.7 percentage points, going from Social Security's 5.3 percent to PSSAs' 7 percent. This will add measurably to the worker's benefit. In no way should this be construed as a tax hike. It is just the opposite. Workers are being liberated from an onerous tax—for which tens of millions of workers are expected to receive little, even if Social Security were to keep its promises—and finally permitted to invest their own money for their own retirement in their own personal account and not pay someone else's way. Seven percent will work to the advantage of both young and older workers. Young workers with a lion's share of their careers ahead of them will see their PSSAs grow to several million dollars.

A few calculations show how much better a 7 percent PSSA contribution is compared to 5.3 percent. A young worker, like twenty-three-year-old Jennifer Median, putting 5.3 percent of wages into a PSSA between now and retirement at age sixty-seven in 2040, would accumulate around $1.6 million. Not bad at all, but 7 percent does much better. The same worker investing 7 percent will have a final balance that is 32 percent greater, $2.1 million![5]

For a worker who invests in a PSSA throughout his or her career, the annuity funded by the PSSA would not only top Target 42—the target of replacing 42 percent of the final work year's earnings—but would also almost duplicate the worker's final salary!

The PSSA that Jennifer opens this year, which will grow to $2.1 million by 2040, will fund an annuity that pays an initial annual benefit of $195,000. And that will replace 96 percent of her earnings in the year before retirement. The pay-as-you-go Social Security system cannot come close.[6]

Future entrants to the labor force, going directly into a PSSA, could expect similar results at retirement after a full career. They will surpass Target 42 by a wide margin. Workers as old as thirty-one, enrolling this year in a PSSA, would probably have enough time to reach a replacement level of more than 60 percent.[7]

The 7 percent rate will help older workers, particularly baby boomers, gain precious ground, despite their late entry into a PSSA. A middle-aged baby boomer, like forty-one-year-old John Boomer, would accumulate some $273,000, almost three-quarters of his Target 42. The balance needed would come from the Social Security benefits earned from contributions prior to joining a PSSA, but only that portion needed to reach Target 42. John Boomer's Social Security payroll contributions through last

Social Security Tax (OASI) Rates Compared to PSSA Savings/Tax Rates

	OASI TAX RATES	PSSA SAVINGS RATE
EMPLOYEE	5.3%	7.0%
EMPLOYER	5.3%	**PSSA TAX RATE** 6.0%

Source: Author's PRA Plan and Social Security Administration

Chart 32

year have earned him $22,764 in benefits starting in 2021. He would need and receive less than half of that to close the gap with his PSSA benefits to reach his Target 42.[8] Since he would not draw the full amount from Social Security, he would save Social Security and American taxpayers money, but he would not be receiving less than he would had he stayed with Social Security.

Bob, the first-year boomer from chapter 2, now age fifty, could still accumulate more than $88,000, a third of the way to his Target 42.[9] Just as with John Boomer, the balance needed to reach Target 42 for Bob and everyone else joining a PSSA would come from the Social Security benefits they earned prior to joining their PSSA. Maximizing the PSSA's bottom line for these boomers means fewer Social Security benefits will be needed to bring them to their Target 42, helping to drive down Social Security's liability and deficits.

An added benefit of the 7 percent contribution rate is that it pushes the choice cutoff age higher than the other rates that were considered. At 5.3 percent, a worker would likely have to open a PSSA by age thirty-three ultimately to attain Target 42 from a PSSA alone. Six percent nudges the breakpoint to age thirty-five. But 7 percent generates enough compound growth to permit someone as old as thirty-seven to open a PSSA this year and achieve their Target 42.[10] The thirty-seven-year-old worker opening a PSSA this year and contributing 7 percent of salary could, with compound interest, retire at age sixty-seven with a PSSA balance of $465,000, funding a Target 42 annuity paying annual benefits the first year of $42,321.[11]

By pushing the cutoff age as high as thirty-seven, a 7 percent contribution rate saves the nation many billions of dollars over time because millions of retirees draw less Social Security benefits to reach Target 42, meaning a lower deficit and less to be funded by bonds.

PSSA-PLUS ADVANTAGE

With a mandatory 7 percent PSSA contribution, a worker's total contribution to a PSSA can reach 14 percent. By taking advantage of the optional PSSA-Plus, a worker can match his or her mandatory contribution, doubling the investment. By putting another 7 percent into PSSA-Plus, the twenty-three-year-old's total PSSA/PSSA-Plus balance could top $4 million by retirement; a thirty-year-old's, $2 million; a forty-year-old's, $600,000; a fifty-year-old's, $177,000; a fifty-five-year-old's, $78,000; and a sixty-year-old's, $25,000.[12] These sums are based on contributions from average wages.

PSSA-Plus would also prove particularly advantageous to couples. The mandatory PSSA balance that a single person could accumulate becomes twice that for a married couple with combined accounts, and four times the lone PSSA balance if both members of the couple took full advantage of PSSA-Plus. The PSSA that twenty-three-year-old Jennifer Median opens this year would top $2 million by retirement in 2040. She would double that amount by taking full advantage of PSSA-Plus. Single and still at home where the rent is minimal, Jennifer expects to marry one day. At retirement time, the combination of *her* PSSA and PSSA-Plus accounts and *his* PSSA and PSSA-Plus accounts could have a balance in the year 2040 of $8 million, which would fund annuities that would be far greater than their wages ever were.

PSSA-Plus would be especially valuable to baby boomers and older workers. Remember that PSSA-Plus will not penalize earned Social Security benefits. PSSA-Plus effectively responds to economist Douglas Bernheim's challenge to baby boomers to save more—much more—for their retirement.

More than three-quarters of baby boomers are married, including people who married after a divorce. Since most baby boom wives work, two workers funding two PSSAs and two PSSA-Plus accounts promise rapid wealth accumulation. PSSA will benefit not only today's workers in retirement, but also their children, because the plan will lighten the burden and brighten the future of younger generations, who are freed from having to prop up Social Security for their elders.

The 7/6 combination also directly helps to lower Social Security's present value deficit. Instead of leaving Social Security with a present value deficit of $2.7 trillion, under the 7/6 PSSA combo that obligation falls immediately by $1.6 trillion—to $1.1 trillion.[13] That sum can be financed prudently and in full by bonds that we should have no difficulty paying off. So too Social Security's annual cash-flow deficits can eventually be driven down and eliminated, and replaced by surpluses.

By way of comparison, keeping both worker and employer contributions at 5.3 percent would push up the current liability to $3.1 trillion.[14] That liability would eventually come down, but we want to solve the Social Security crisis, not exacerbate it.

Why not raise the employer's rate to 7 percent, just like the employee's? Simple. The employee's 7 percent contribution goes to his PSSA investment. It is not a tax, it is an investment. It benefits both the *employee* and the economy. But the employer's portion is not an investment. It still goes to the pay-as-you-go Social Security system. It is a pure tax. Increasing the employer's portion from 5.3 percent to 7 percent would amount to a 32 percent tax increase. The trade-off is reducing the deficit while not unreasonably taxing labor. A 6 percent employer tax, in our view, achieves both goals.

With the PSSA plan, the 6 percent rate on employers should hold firm and usher Social Security toward eventual shut-down—after which the employer tax would be eliminated. Compared to alternatives, 6 percent would be both palatable and beneficial to most employers.

Here's how it might play out. Under 7 and 6, the money needed to pay out Target 42 benefits from Social Security would peak around the year 2037 at $2.4 trillion per year. After that Social Security payments would drop sharply. Only five years later, around 2042, Social Security would be running a cash sur-plus. In four years, the surplus would top $1 trillion. By 2050 the surplus would grow by $2.2 trillion per year.[15] The last par-tial payment of Target 42 benefits would be made around the year 2060. In that year, the system's cash-flow *surplus* would be $5 trillion.[16] The old system would be officially shut down.

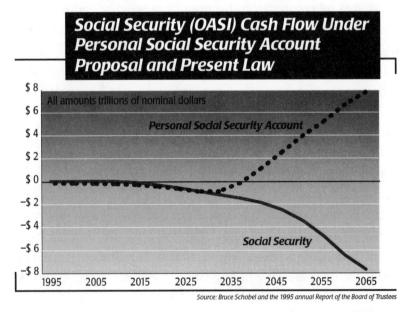

Source: Bruce Schobel and the 1995 annual Report of the Board of Trustees

Chart 33

What if we stay with the current system? Well then, in 2060 Social Security would have an annual cash-flow *deficit* of $4.5 trillion, and growing.[17] That's right, $4.5 trillion a year in the red.

Actually, either vision is a convincing argument for enacting a PSSA program.

EITHER WAY, 7/6 SAVES THE SYSTEM

The truth is anyone staying in Social Security would derive one enormous benefit because of the PSSA plan: a solvent Social Security system. Instead of collapsing, Social Security would continue to pay benefits, even as the system winds down, its payout burden reduced by PSSAs.

So why not raise Social Security taxes from 5.3 percent to 7 percent on those who stay in Social Security? After all, that is what PSSA joiners will pay.

Once again the answer is that Social Security payments are taxes, not investments. Raising the tax rate on those who stay in the system would mean they would get even less of a return on their tax dollars. That is neither fair nor politically practical.

Inertia, skepticism, or closeness to retirement may induce some workers to stay with Social Security. For whatever reason, those who remain behind will have to pay only the prevailing system rate.

We must also remember the thirty-eight million people who are already collecting Social Security retirement benefits—parents, grandparents, neighbors we all know. Sixty-three percent of Social Security recipients rely on their benefits for half or more of their retirement income. Twenty-six percent rely on Social Security for 90 percent or more.[18] We *declare unequivo-*

cally that their benefits should not be touched. Their benefits, in fact, will acquire added protection by the PSSA plan.

And the protection and enhancement of retirement assets is, in the end, our real goal. We recognize the great value demonstrated through the years by the Social Security program. We know that it has done a great deal of good for tens of millions of Americans; that it has done nothing less than provide many retirees with the security they needed in their later years. While we honor what Social Security has accomplished, we also recognize that shifting demographics demand that we make changes in order to help provide security for all retirees.

HUMMING WIRES: WHERE THE MONEY GOES

Computerization, automated deposit, and debit techniques will help send the billions of dollars gathered at three rates from one source in two directions. The PSSAs' 7 percent will go to the chosen PSSA investment manager, while the employer's 6 percent and the stay-behind worker's 10.6 percent will go to the U.S. Treasury. Employers will be responsible for withholding and routing employee contributions, just as they do now with Social Security taxes, pension contributions, and income withholding. A PSSA adds only the transfer cycle to financial institutions.

Computerized data processing already helps employers in New York City, Washington, D.C., and elsewhere handle withholding of local taxes at different rates—one rate for city residents and another for commuters.

With the proper software and necessary data entered, it matters little if a company's employees choose one or several financial institutions to manage their PSSAs.

CHAPTER FIFTEEN

THE WAVE-TO-SAVE PICKS UP SPEED

B ETWEEN LISTENING TO Country and Western tapes and hunting for Rush Limbaugh on local radio, long-haul truckers for J. B. Hunt Transport are apt to slip in a cassette to hear the latest financial poop on the company's 401(k) pension plan and how to use its benefit to full advantage. "Don't get lost on the road to retirement," warns one tape.

After hearing the tape and attending a seminar at a company depot, forty-three-year-old Gary Brown signed up for the 401(k) plan in 1994. "I want to be able to live comfortably," Brown told *Business Week*.[1] He puts 4 percent of his salary into the plan; his company, 2 percent.

At trendy, youth-oriented E! Entertainment Television, where the average staff age is thirty, workers get updates on E!'s 401(k) plan plus financial advice via voice- and e-mail and posters touting the company's "Stash Your Cash" campaign. "It's a nice, secure feeling that I won't have to live in a cardboard box in my old age," says E!'s Robert Sheiffele, age thirty-four, who's taken his company's campaign advice and joined the saving brigade.[2]

Significantly larger, the more traditional General Motors runs periodic sessions at its factories and offices around the nation to educate employees from assembly-line workers to corporate executives about their benefits, including 401(k)s and retirement planning.[3]

Business generally is stepping up efforts to help employees get top money mileage on the road to retirement. Workers at every turn along the way are asking tough questions, pondering alternative routes, and making the savings decision. The General Motors turnout has been so overwhelming that GM has held more than one thousand sessions so far.[4]

From Wall Street to Main Street, financial institutions are also mounting more of their own retirement seminars and multimedia campaigns. One example: Merrill Lynch, which on its own initiative designated April as "National Savings Month," teamed with the *Wall Street Journal* to develop an interactive crash course on saving and retirement investment for students.[5] Merrill Lynch also publishes *Retirement Advisor,* a monthly newsletter that tracks markets, offers investment strategies, and reports on relevant legislation in Washington for its clients.

IRONING OUT
REGULATORY ROADBLOCKS

Meanwhile, Congress finally appears to be moving toward genuine reforms to untangle long-standing legislative and regulatory roadblocks to more individual saving for retirement and adequate company funding of pensions. Hoping to pressure legislators to act, Merrill Lynch offers a toll-free number giving names and addresses of congressional representatives who callers can lobby for tax and pension reform.[6]

This building wave-to-save effort signals a new realism and understanding of the obstacles on the road to retirement, including the Social Security crisis—a major threat to secure retirement, but not the only one.

Even though PSSAs can successfully replace Social Security, the idea of retirement as a three-legged stool still applies. The other two legs—voluntary savings accounts and pensions—still need attention. While the focus of this book is Social Security and the PSSA solution, we offer some suggestions on what to do about the other legs.

To stabilize the stool's other legs will require a major reappraisal by government, employers, the financial community, and individual workers. We believe this to be the opportune time to present the PSSA idea, to examine and correct America's savings and pension policies, to create a reorganizing synergy that will permit them to work harmoniously rather than at cross-purposes.

This reappraisal must be an inclusive, cooperative venture.

The following are some key items we believe must be on the agenda:

- ❖ Employers must expand efforts to inform and educate workers about pension options and benefits, personal savings, and other ways to provide for retirement.
- ❖ Individual workers and retirees must not depend on others to do what they should do themselves. They must start saving more, sooner, and must invest wisely by diversifying to protect their nest eggs.

SAVE IT OR LOSE IT

Americans simply must save more—and be permitted to save more—to secure their own future and ultimately the nation's. Yet, achieving that goal has been made unnecessarily difficult by the politics of cross purposes, a give-and-take-back game that baffles and demoralizes Americans. Nothing captures the syndrome more vividly than the puzzling case of IRAs—introduced in 1975 to salve concerns about Social Security and the half of the workforce not covered by company pensions. Qualifying workers could make tax-deductible contributions—initially up to $1,500 a year; later, up to $2,000.

The regulations, eventually extended to spouses not covered by pensions, again were amended effective in 1982, making virtually any worker eligible to invest something in IRAs, with contributions and investment earnings tax deferred. The roaring success of IRAs proved that Americans were ready and willing to save on taxes and do something about retirement. Then Congress changed the rules.

"Instead of seeing this as a sign of success, Congress decided to see it as a problem and, in the Tax Reform Act of 1986, severely limited the tax incentives associated with IRAs," recalls Dorcas Hardy, the commissioner of Social Security at the time. "Not surprisingly, people are now putting less money into IRAs—although it's still a very substantial program. And Congress continues to scold the public for a low savings rate."[7]

Congress enacted similar counterproductive tax policy in 1987: it dramatically cut the amount that employers could contribute tax-free to their company pension funds to cover the benefits of future retirees. The same Congress that created the Pension Benefit Guaranty Corporation—to tax employers and guard against pension failure—undermines pensions by taking more in taxes on good pension plans.

In 1987 "Congress made it illegal for companies to put enough money into their pension funds to make sure they'll have enough assets to pay promised benefits. Bizarre?" Craig S. Karpel, founder of Future Elders of America, asked rhetorically. Bizarre, but instructive, perhaps: "The trade-off: more revenue for the federal government in the short term, less retirement income safety for you in the long term," Karpel concludes in his book *The Retirement Myth*.[8]

"A better future for America can be secured if the country embarks on the course of long-term reform of our entitlement and tax system. We can help Americans save and invest in themselves and the country," said the Bipartisan Commission on Entitlement and Tax Reform in its 1994 Interim Report to the President.[9]

And we had better move toward reform fast: the national debt currently stands at close to $5 trillion,[10] on top of Social Security's separate total liability of $7.5 trillion.[11] While the economy outpaced debt between 1951 and 1979, the reverse has occurred since then. By 1994 the federal debt had swollen to 52 percent of GDP, dragging on economic growth.[12]

Meanwhile, the net national savings rate dropped from 7.1 percent in the 1970s to 1.8 percent in the 1990s. According to the Congressional Budget Office, federal deficits were responsible for more than half the savings decline; business and personal savings each accounted for one-quarter.[13]

Real remedial action is the only antidote. In addition to PSSAs there are other steps, not dependent on PSSAs, that could be taken to help Americans retire securely. Some of what we call for involves broad, sweeping changes; others involve more targeted change. But we believe the overwhelming majority of the action items we suggest involve common sense more than anything else.

Action Item 1. Reauthorize full deductibility of IRA contributions and provide Americans with more incentives for personal savings.

Congress should act on proposals to restore IRA deductibility up to $4,000 per year by eliminating a minefield of exclusions imposed by the Tax Reform Act of 1986. In the last two sessions, Congress also has debated the concept of a Super IRA, in which the contributions are taxed but earnings on withdrawal are not. Workers could invest in either a regular or Super IRA, up to $2,000 a year. Introduced by Senator William V. Roth, Jr., (R–Del.) and Senator John Breaux (D–La.), the Roth–Breaux Super IRA would also permit a nonworking spouse to invest up to $2,000.

Beyond IRAs, we believe the current tax structure's overriding problem is that it punishes savers and actually encourages consumption. That could be reversed by a family tax credit, cuts in capital gains taxes, or expanded IRAs. "Instead of viewing tax incentives for saving as socially regressive in intent—to benefit the rich—we should see them as progressive—the key to upward mobility for the masses," contends Paul Hewitt of the National Taxpayer's Union Foundation. "Instead of viewing savers as selfish, we must recognize that they are committing socially responsible acts of self-denial that enable others to earn a decent living."[14]

Not only do workers today lack incentives to save, they are actually penalized, and repeatedly, for saving. After first paying payroll and income taxes, a worker who puts money into a savings account, certificate of deposit, or stocks is again taxed on corporate earnings, dividends paid from the after-tax earnings, and interest income. If stock is sold at a profit, the worker again pays a tax—capital gains. In fact the worker is taxed even if his or her paper "profit" reflects only inflation, so what is left after taxes is less, in real terms, than the original investment! And finally, when the worker dies, his or her heirs are hit with estate or gift taxes. With all these disincentives, it is no wonder Americans save as little as they do.

For two decades, Congress has bounced the maximum capital gains tax rate around as if dribbling a basketball. The maximum rate on long-term gains currently stands at 28 percent, which is down from 35 percent in 1978, but up from 20 percent in 1981.[15] Seeking to avoid the tax, investors are staying put in old investments or moving into tax-free investments. "In all, economists at the Joint Economic Committee estimate, $1.5 trillion in capital gains are locked up in the economy, awaiting a reduction in the capital gains tax," reports Senator Connie Mack (R–Fla.) committee chairman.[16] Proposals in Congress now would cut the maximum rate to 19.8 percent, much lower for most taxpayers.

The most aggressive pro-savings plan of all, the Unlimited Savings Allowance Tax (USA Tax) Act, co-sponsored by Senators Sam Nunn (D–Ga.) and Pete Domenici (R–N. Mex.), would provide a full and unlimited tax deferral on all savings until withdrawal. In effect every American could have a no-limit IRA or 401(k).

Action Item 2. Congress must permit employers to increase pension funding.

In the legislation enacted in 1982 and 1986, Congress dramatically raised taxes on pension contributions by employers, perversely encouraging them to put off contributions and making it much harder to meet their obligations in future years. To the contrary, pensions need to be adequately prefunded, so that companies won't become bankrupt trying to fund the shortfall in the coming decades as aging baby boomers start to collect. The longer that Washington and employers delay, the more difficult it will be to fund those pensions.

There are significant pension reform proposals pending in Congress that would simplify regulations, reduce administrative costs, and make more pensions portable. But portability raises the old urge-to-splurge demon: only 63 percent of workers said they would reinvest their lump-sum payments after a job change, an Employee Benefit Research Institute (EBRI)/Gallup poll found—even in the face of tax penalties for rollover failure.

While we strongly oppose overregulation, some rules of the road are sensible. Reasoned restrictions on what workers can do with pension funds, such as disincentives for early withdrawal or spendthrift consumption, are not out of line. Tax incentives for responsible retirement planning were created to avoid the building of such safety net systems as Social Security, not to fund preretirement consumption.

Action Item 3. Workers and retirees must become more informed, astute investors and students of successful retirement planning.

Campaigns, such as General Motors' and E! Entertainment's, to educate workers on their pension potential are getting results. Yet, even as more workers enroll, too many cheat themselves. Over half do not contribute the maximum to their 401(k) plans; nine of every ten workers leaving pension plans don't reinvest their distributions in other retirement plans; one in four workers plans to use 401(k) savings for a house or a child's education—not retirement.[17]

We sympathize—and empathize—with workers today: with plenty to do on the job alone, modern life requires that workers study up on arcana such as defined benefit versus defined contribution pension plans, annuities, equities, bonds, and investment contracts. But in today's economic battleground, knowing the economic ropes—and the knots and tangles—is critical.

Efficiently organized information abounds in the marketing barrage of brokerage houses, banks, and mutual funds. Computer programs can walk you through the basics and can even calculate your personal needs and investment alternatives. Libraries bulge with books on investment and retirement planning. And we offer our own advice in the appendix. The problem, obviously, is not a dearth of information but of making the commitment and time to negotiate some of the tricky curves on the pension and investment roadways. Ultimately, individual experience is the best teacher, because it's your money and your future at risk.

Action Item 4. Just as individuals must plan for the future, so too must financial institutions.

Creativity and clarity are going to give brokers and bankers and insurance companies the edge in the PSSA era. Many of the pension and investment products, policies, and strategies, based on old assumptions, will not cut it in the twenty-first century. The buyer of financial products is moving downstream from the corporate executive to the individual investor. The empowerment of the individual will forever change the financial landscape. The financial industry should rethink, redesign, and refine flexible products and simplified services, giving investors creative, pension-building strategies that take full advantage of widening domestic and international market opportunities.

Americans need more hybrid pension products, combining the best elements of defined benefit plans and defined contribution plans, such as lifestyle funds in which a particular investment mix matches worker's age and risk tolerance. To gain superior PSSA performance, younger workers can tolerate higher risk and more equity investment. As a worker ages and approaches retirement, less volatile fixed income investments may become more appropriate. Only 9 percent of defined contribution plans' assets trickle into flexible lifestyle funds. But here is where the next wave-to-save should be building.

Within the next five years, defined contribution plans such as 401(k)s are expected to account for 60 percent of the nation's primary pension policies.[18] The shift, begun two decades ago, appears to be driven at least partly by negative reaction to the Employee Retirement Income Security Act of 1974 (ERISA). While Congress thought that ERISA would strengthen defined benefit plans, the law dumped more regulations and cost on employers, fueling a move to defined contribution plans.

A 1994 study by Merrill Lynch & Co. found that "administrative costs of complying with complex pension regulations have unfortunately discouraged many businesses (especially small businesses) from providing adequate pension coverage to employees."[19] In 1991 an employer sponsoring a defined benefits plan for fifteen or fewer workers incurred regulatory costs of $455 per participant. Comparable expenses for a defined contribution plan were half.[20]

In the era of downsizing and job-hopping, defined contribution plans have the advantage of being not only portable but also tax-preferred. When leaving a company with a defined contribution plan, an employee can collect a lump-sum payment that can be reinvested in a new retirement account.

In contrast, defined benefit plans are not nearly as portable. Anyone who leaves before vesting runs the risk of receiving either no benefits or only a portion. The average worker loses 15 percent of potential pension benefits because of job turnover, according to a 1993 study published by the Upjohn Institute. The loss can be as high as 30 percent or more for some workers.[21]

THE INHERITANCE BUBBLE:
A CUSHION FOR THE STOOL

The retirement stool, once steadied and strengthened, could well use a cushion in the form of inheritance, no longer limited to wealthy families.

Baby boomers and post-boomers stand at the receiving end of a multitrillion dollar inheritance from their more frugal parents, whose careers and housing investments racked up significant gains during a period of steady growth and appreciation. A 1993 Congressional Budget Office report calculates that unimpeded inheritance could double or triple the current wealth of baby boomers over the next several decades.

"If the surviving spouse of the median elderly couple holds $100,000 at the time of death and each elderly couple has three children, then the median amount inherited per child would be about $30,000. Married-couple households would inherit $60,000," noted the report, *Baby Boomers in Retirement: An Early Perspective.*[22] While far from enough on which to retire, such a legacy would prove helpful in feathering the nest.

The Congressional Budget Office's good news may understate the amount of the windfall, because the report used only households in which the head was sixty-five to seventy-four years old. Cornell University economists Robert B. Avery and Michael S. Rendall estimate that between 1990 and 2040, parents will be leaving their baby boomer children upwards of $10.4 trillion (1989 dollars).[23] That whopping windfall may shrink slightly because neither study factors in what parents

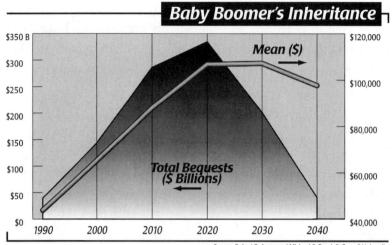

Chart 34

might leave to other relatives, friends, or charities rather than their children. Nor does either study reflect life expectancy gains since 1989; i.e., longer life means less to leave heirs.

HOME EQUITY: THE NEST IN THE NEST EGG

Curiously, economists and others often do not consider the biggest asset most Americans have when sizing up retirement: the nest in nest egg—the home equity that two-thirds of households own. "Housing wealth accounts for more than half of all wealth for the median household (aged 55 to 74)," notes *Baby Boomers in Retirement*.[24] Yet many studies exclude home equity in totting up retirement nest eggs because of home equity's lack of liquidity. And even retirees can't live out their days holed up in recreational vehicles (RVs). Nevertheless, home equity for baby boomers and post-boomers will be substantial and can be tapped by downsizing to smaller, less expensive homes.

A 1994 study by EBRI finds that baby boomers' retirement income would go farther if they leveraged their home equity. If home equity is added to their other savings, boomers are currently saving 84 percent of what would be needed to maintain their living standard, according to EBRI.[25]

"To the extent that boomers are willing to tap into this resource to fund their retirement, they would appear at this early stage to be in pretty good shape," contends Dallas Salisbury, president of EBRI.[26]

Action Item 5. Home ownership—the American dream—must be encouraged and pursued.

Reduction of the federal deficit will help lower mortgage rates. And genuine tax reform that encourages Americans to save and invest will also generate money with which more families can make a downpayment on achieving the American Dream of buying a home. New mortgage terms and vehicles can further boost ownership and enhance liquidity.

One way that retirees now have of getting equity from their homes is through a reverse mortgage loan, which provides monthly benefits in return for the bank's taking possession of the house after the deaths of the homeowners. Other alternatives for accessing home equity must and will emerge as demand increases.

More than two-thirds of baby boomers and one-third of post-boomers are already homeowners. Home ownership rates rise with age and will likely continue to do so with these two generations. More than three-quarters of householders over age fifty, including retirees, own their own homes. By 1994 the overall U.S. home ownership rate was 64 percent.[27] That's down from the 1980 peak of 65.6 percent.[28]

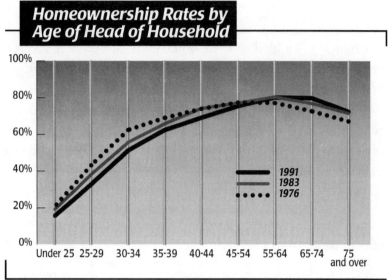

Source: Joint Center for Housing Studies of Harvard University and Bureau of the Census

Chart 35

The State of the Nation's Housing 1995, a report by the Joint Center for Housing Studies of Harvard University, forecasts that "the single-family housing market will be robust throughout the 1990s. In most areas, baby-boom tradeup demand will keep single-family construction going strong. But in particular locations, new niches will open up with the rapid growth of minority and immigrant populations. In others, the strongest growth market will in fact be elderly housing."[29]

The report continues: "To take advantage of these opportunities, builders, lenders, and realtors must carefully assess local market conditions, and particularly the demographic and economic forces that generate new market demand."[30]

While boomers and post-boomers will probably not realize the astounding appreciation experienced by the World War II generation, the younger generations should still fare reasonably well in the real estate market, which remains a sound investment.

CHAPTER SIXTEEN

RETIRING
WITH DIGNITY

W E BELIEVE THAT our plan will help provide America's workers with the retirement security that is fundamental to human dignity and self-respect.

While the PSSA plan is not intended as the only source of retirement income, it's likely to provide the biggest slice of the retirement pie. But how much retirement income is enough? That question has at least 180 million answers—the present number of workers and retirees in the United States.

Computer programs can and will provide a personalized answer for every American. Typically, you'll need retirement income at about 70 percent of what you earned in the last year of employment in order to maintain your standard of living, says a widely accepted formula. Using that benchmark, the combination of the PSSA/PSSA-Plus and other assets will lift almost everyone well above that point.

How much are we getting now? And from where?

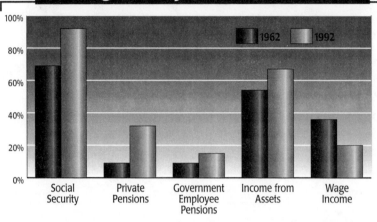

Source: Social Security Administration

Chart 36

About one-third of all retirees (and half of all new retirees) are presently receiving pension benefits. The AARP projects that number will rise to more than 80 percent for the baby boomers.[1] Pensions currently account for 19 percent of the aggregate income of the elderly.[2]

Two out of three seniors have income from assets (interest, dividends, and rental income).[3] The median cash income from assets was $2,356 in 1990.[4] One in five earn something from working after age sixty-five. Their wages account for 17 percent of aggregate income of the senior population.[5]

Two-thirds of American households own their own home; three-quarters of those age sixty-five and older do. And four-fifths of older homeowners have paid off their mortgages.

Despite this rather complicated equation that determines most people's retirement income, adults spend considerably less time planning for their retirement than one might think.

According to information acquired by the Principal Finance Group and reported in the 12 March 1996 issue of *USA Today,* individuals spend on average 9.1 hours *annually* planning for their retirement—one-sixteenth as much time as they spend shopping for clothes.

THE AMERICAN RENAISSANCE

The PSSA plan and all who seize its opportunities will generate dividends far beyond retirement.

In the very process of securing retirement, the nation, its people, its communities, and its economy will be reinvigorated. The success of the PSSA idea will boost savings, increase investment, reduce the long-term deficit, accelerate the growth of national and local economies, and create new jobs and business opportunities.

We have high hopes for the ripple effects of the PSSA plan— above all, to heighten personal liberty and responsibility. The PSSA plan encourages, rewards, and stimulates personal initiative and conveys the notion that people can take hold of their lives and make productive changes—even in adversity.

Social critic Robert Hughes, in his 1993 book *Culture of Complaint: The Fraying of America,* decried what he perceived to be the pervasive cult of victimology in the United States. Instead of believing in and pursuing the American Dream, too many people have acted as though they are victims—either of heartless forces or of their fate. Intentionally or not, a huge government bureaucracy has encouraged dependency with its myriad entitlement programs. It has turned needy constituents into servile advocates and has stifled personal initiative.

Social Security was a product of the Great Depression and the cornerstone of the New Deal. The principles of the PSSA plan can be the keystone of the reborn American Dream: we will look to ourselves—not government—for the shape and texture of our personal destiny and individual dreams, knowing that only our abdication of responsibility makes the government leviathan.

PSSA: FUELING OF PRODUCTIVITY

Deposits flowing into PSSA accounts will pump billions and then trillions of dollars a year into productive investments. Money previously consumed by the government will now be available for business investment.

A larger capital supply means lower borrowing rates for businesses and entrepreneurs wanting to expand, modernize, undertake research and development, or introduce new products or services. And the lower the borrowing rates, the more jobs will be created in those strategic areas and the higher the wages will rise. "When firms have access to cheap capital . . . they invest more in technologies that increase output per worker," and thus wages, observes National Taxpayers Union executive Paul S. Hewitt. Such investments "also create more jobs, since low interest rates make more investments economically viable at the margin."[6]

And he adds: "A manager facing a 3 percent interest rate is far more likely to invest in better plant and equipment than one with a 9 percent cost of capital. This is why capital-intensive industry tends to thrive, and wages tend to rise in countries with high savings rates. Conversely, industry tends to grow more slowly in economies with low savings rates."[7]

In the U.S. today productivity grows at less than 1 percent a year, real wages are stagnant, and unemployment is higher than need be. But an expanding capital supply can increase productivity, revive real wage gains, and push unemployment down.

Enacting the PSSA plan will over time eliminate Social Security's annual deficits and cut its long-range deficit by 60 percent, a savings to the federal government and ultimately the taxpayer.[8]

SPENDING IN RETIREMENT: SECURE IS BEST

In retirement, living expenses drop—often by 30 percent or more. There's no more commuting, no need to buy new office outfits each year, no more expensive lunches or noon deli take-out. But spending doesn't stop. And, not surprising, the financially secure in retirement spend more than the insecure. They will eat out, travel, entertain, play tennis or golf, and generally enjoy themselves more.

Annual expenditures for a sixty-five–plus household averaged $21,322 in 1993. More than $1,800 of that was spent on travel, meals or eating out, and entertainment. Magazines, newspapers, and books rang up another $150.[9]

While we're still years away from people retiring with PSSAs, the power of retiree spending today can be seen in familiar senior watering holes such as Florida and Arizona. Nineteen percent of Florida's population is aged sixty-five or older, the same proportion that the country as a whole will reach around the year 2025 as the last baby boomers settle into their retirement RVs. In just one month, more than $1.4 billion in retirement benefits now flows from Social Security to Florida.[10] While Floridians grumble about seniors slowing traffic, they are a powerful driver of the state's economy. Their clout can only climb in Florida or any state when the checks arriving in the future are the more generous PSSA benefits.

And as aging Americans pioneer new boom towns, senior spending sparks the economy in unlikely new oases such as Cleveland, Georgia.

Rural Cleveland, in the northern end of Georgia, used to

be a struggling tobacco farming community. Now the cash crop is retirees, attracted there by the clean air, lakes, mountains, and lack of congestion. "This place was nothing. Retirees are helping things now, taxes are coming in," notes a Cleveland native who sells preserves at his roadside stand. "Most people don't want to go back to what it was. They want to see building."[11]

The influx of retirees has spawned a building boom, transformed the local economy, and expanded job opportunities, from clerks at the new malls to accountants and physicians.

TRENDS: THE GRAPES OF WRATH IN REVERSE

The same thing has happened in Clinton, Oklahoma, a scenic, lake-dappled spot deserted during Dust Bowl days for California. Many of those transplants have come home to retire, increasing demand for goods and services and creating jobs. An official at the local Chamber of Commerce described what's happened as "The Grapes of Wrath in Reverse."[12]

The ones who have come to Florida, as well as Cleveland and Clinton, tend to have disposable incomes that are at or above the national average. When people do start retiring with PSSAs, these communities and ones like them will not have to jump-start the Chamber of Commerce to attract financially secure retirees from elsewhere. Plenty of financially secure seniors will probably be living there already.

CHAPTER SEVENTEEN

FORGING COALITIONS TO MAKE PSSAS HAPPEN

"*Modern Maturity,* the magazine of people doing 50 and over, has just moved into the fast lane," crowed the national ad in major publications late last year.[1]

The once-clunky magazine of the influential AARP had undergone a major makeover. When the bandages came off with the January/February 1996 issue, there was a slick, provocative new forum for AARP. On the cover were the visages of actress Diane Keaton, singer/songwriter Bruce Springsteen, basketball great Kareem Abdul-Jabbar, and Hollywood producer/director Steven Spielberg. Above their heads a bold three-line teaser proclaimed:

BOO!

MERS

The Babies Face Fifty

The table of contents listed four stories as part of the "MM Special: The Boomers Are Coming." One was a piece on the tumultuous 1960s with reminiscences by Tom Hayden, as well as former Vice President Dan Quayle, among others.

The next issue of *Modern Maturity,* featuring Miss Manners on the cover with her "up-to-date rules of etiquette" for the 1990s inside, contained a lively, engaging mix of lifestyle, entertainment, financial, and political articles. Lest anyone miss whom the magazine was trying to recruit to their readership, one lifestyle piece explored "The Big Five-Oh."

The times they are a-changin', indeed, and with them *Modern Maturity,* and its patron, the powerful AARP.

The magazine's makeover was no coincidence, coming as it did just as the first wave of baby boomers began turning fifty. The oldest baby boomers, born in 1946, now are eligible to join the thirty-three-million–member AARP.

Baby boomers will do what they have done throughout their lives—overwhelm or challenge institutions and people first encountering their presence. AARP, long a bulwark against tampering with Social Security, will become an agent of change in the systemic struggle as more and more members demand and get action that could include the PSSA plan.

Other developments and other key people make today an opportune time for free-wheeling debate on retooling Social Security or enacting a bold innovation such as the PSSA plan. As the 1996 campaigns and election conclude, America's legislators will have a mandate to legislate reform in the true interest of the American people, rather than maintain the status quo. With a White House secure for four years, the president can seize the initiative, break with past pessimism, and lead the nation in a bold, hopeful, new direction.

Key members of Congress are well versed in the problems of Social Security and the need for reform, such as Senator Bob Kerrey (D–Neb.), Senator Phil Gramm (R–Tex.), Representative Charles Stenholm (D–Tex.), and Representative Jim Kolbe (R–Ariz.). Kerrey and the retiring Senator Alan Simpson (R–Wyo.) advanced their prescriptions for overhauling Social Security without being electrocuted politically—proof that Social Security may no longer be the third rail of politics. Stenholm and Kolbe head a forty-member House caucus studying the concept of partial privatization of Social Security.

Likely to light a fire under any legislators waffling on reform will be PAC 20/20, a political action committee formed just last year. "Our organization advocates looking clearly at this issue *now* to ensure that we have a viable system in the next century," says Christian Klein, PAC 20/20's young founder. "PAC 20/20 will actively support the election of candidates for federal office who have demonstrated a commitment to reforming our nation's Social Security system."[2]

COALITION BUILDING

A president and legislators who propose a PSSA plan as the appropriate solution to twenty-first century retirement can count on facing what Franklin Roosevelt faced in introducing so dramatic a social change. Ultimately, however, the PSSA plan will require bipartisan support and overwhelming congressional passage of enabling legislation.

Such legislation would surely foment a dogfight, months of hearings, lobbying, congressional wrangling, and town-hall debate. The news media should have a field day. Expert witnesses would no doubt include people from AARP, the young

people's Third Millennium, the National Taxpayers Union
Foundation, the Committee for Economic Development, and
the General Accounting Office, among others.

As authors of the PSSA plan, we would welcome the opportunity to testify and would be available to discuss the PSSA
details in any appropriate forum.

Others whose perspective and experience would be enlight-
ening include Dorcas Hardy, commissioner of Social Security
from 1986 to 1989, and Bruce Schobel, a Social Security actuary from 1979 to 1988. They speak with an insider's knowledge
of Social Security—how it works, how it's supposed to work,
and how it doesn't work.

There's also Dallas L. Salisbury, president of EBRI, who has
researched and written widely on Social Security and pensions;
John C. Goodman, president of the National Center for Policy
Analysis; and think-tank scholar Peter J. Ferrara, author of
Social Security: The Inherent Contradiction.

We do not propose limiting the debate to these people. In
fact, we do not know what any of these people or groups would
say, except that they understand the urgent need for major
reform. We expect reflexive opposition to the PSSA plan, particularly from Social Security advocates who cling to the notion
that it can be repaired by further fine-tuning. Robert Myers,
chief actuary of the Social Security Administration from 1947 to
1970, has written incisively about Social Security staffers seeking to protect and expand the system "with almost a religious
zeal" and described how "some civil servants feel it their obligation and duty to work with the opposition so as to achieve
what they consider desirable goals" to defeat partisan attempts
to reform or reduce their pet programs.[3]

Such opposition will only heighten the contrast between the

crippled Social Security system and the revitalizing PSSA program. Fairly examined, PSSAs will be revealed to be far superior to Social Security and other historical alternatives. Certainly we need, at the very least, frank and open discussion, tough questions, and straight answers, which may not have occurred prior to Social Security's enactment in 1935.

Historian Michael E. Schiltz, who reviewed polling data between 1936 and 1944, concluded that while public support for Social Security was high, misconceptions abounded. "As a consequence, it remains forever moot whether during the Depression the public understood or endorsed the principal of social insurance," concluded Schiltz.[4]

Six decades later the stakes are higher, the public much more skeptical and aware. We can be sure that workers and retirees this time around are going to be demanding solid information and sharp answers on Social Security, the PSSA plan, and other proposed reforms.

THE DREAM COME TRUE

Our dream would be that sometime before the turn of the century, you'll see a certain photograph on the nightly news, then the front pages of America's 1,600 daily newspapers the next day, and a week later in *Time, Newsweek,* and *U.S. News.*

The color photo will feature a personnel manager shaking hands with a grinning employee, maybe Jennifer Median or possibly one of your children or ours, opening up the very first PSSA. Whoever it is, whatever the age, he or she will be randomly selected for historic immortality by a computer somewhere from among the few million people who line up on the first day of PSSA registration and will be given PSSA #000-00-0001.

The picture is sure to run in tandem with a grainy black-and-white shot taken in January 1940 of sixty-five-year-old Ida Mae Fuller, when she received the first monthly benefit check issued by Social Security.

APPENDIX

B Y NOW WE hope that this book has made clear our belief that there is a pressing need for retirement system reform—involving far more private investment—in the United States and in other countries around the world.

No matter how powerful the arguments for reform are and how promising the Personal Social Security Accounts (PSSAs) we suggest may be, such dramatic change will take time to enact. Meanwhile, we hope our readers can and will take action to prepare for their own retirement needs.

The best way to start is by doing just what you're doing now—reading. Bookstores and public libraries are overflowing with fine books on personal investing and financial planning. We urge you to read up on the subject, formulate your own goals, and then seek advice from a financial professional on how to develop a personal plan to meet those goals.

As investment professionals—and investors ourselves—we

would like to leave you with just a few well-tested "rules of thumb" that have served us and our customers well.

SIX GOLDEN RULES OF RETIREMENT INVESTING

1. Start investing early.

The sooner you start investing the better. The power of compounding—the "gains on gains" that reinvested interest and dividends can earn—is truly awesome. Time is money, indeed. Consider this: a person who saves $1,000 a year from age twenty-five to age thirty-five and then stops after just those ten years will accumulate far more money by retirement at age sixty than someone who starts saving the same amount every year at age thirty-five and keeps on saving for twenty-five years up to retirement age. Even if you're older than twenty-five, there's no time to waste. So save—and invest—as much as you can afford. If your company offers a 401(k) or other investment plan, take full advantage of it. If there is no company plan, save on your own. Counting on the Social Security system alone is risky.

2. Be aggressive.

Most people tend, understandably, to be wary of the fluctuations of the stock market and to shy away from risk. That's almost always a mistake—especially for younger investors. Common stocks, which most people view as "risky" or "volatile" investments, have, as we've seen, a longtime track record of returning more than most "safe" investments like bank CDs, bonds, or insurance annuities. Remember, from 1926 to 1995—right through wars, the Great Depression, the OPEC oil shocks, and the "crash" of 1987—U.S. common stocks produced a compound total return of 10.54 percent—enough to make any steady stock buyer comfortable, and perhaps even wealthy, in old age. So take a long-term view. "Stocks will fluctuate," as J. P. Morgan said. But over time, the returns they offer are both large and reliable. So, be aggressive—appropriately so—as we elaborate in the next three rules.

3. Diversify.

Picking individual stocks—or simply buying your own company's stock through your savings plan—can be very lucrative. But concentrating your investments in one or a few stocks can also be very risky. It is far better to invest in a broadly diversified, global portfolio of stocks, bonds, and mutual funds. Spreading your investments over a variety of industries—even nations—tends to reduce fluctuations and spread risk across space and time. Perhaps the single easiest and most popular way to diversify is to buy stock and bond mutual funds that pool your investments and let the professional money managers do your diversification for you. Buying mutual funds is one way to follow this rule's core advice: don't put all of your nest eggs in one basket.

4. Dollar-cost average.

Picking highs and lows in financial marketplaces is a common fantasy of success that few but the most gifted—and lucky—investors achieve. If you are just beginning to invest, it's better to move in steadily, say, with a fixed amount of money per month—and then keep on investing the same amount or more month-in, month-out over the years. Use direct payroll deductions or bank transfers to stay on track. By the same token, it's better to withdraw the capital from your retirement funds after retirement in a disciplined way, a way that makes your money last as long as you expect to live. Don't plunge in and out. Don't panic or grow euphoric. Don't try to buy low or sell high.

5. Act your age.

As important as it is to be aggressive, it's equally important to ratchet risk down carefully as you approach—and pass—your target retirement age. Shift your portfolio gradually, dollar-cost averaging all the way, from growth stocks, to high-dividend blue chips, to fixed-income bonds that can provide you with reliable investment income after you've stopped collecting a paycheck. Some call this "lifestyle" investing. We say: act your age.

6. Have a secure home base.

The liquid financial assets in your investment portfolio may form the core of your retirement income plan. But they are only part of what you'll need for genuine security. Life, health, and disability insurance are also essential. So is a place to live that you can afford, manage, and—most of all—enjoy. Over the past few decades, as the huge baby boom generation came of home-buying age, there was an unprecedented surge in American home values that has only partly retreated since the recession of the early 1990s. Given the size of subsequent "cohorts" of the population, that kind of huge "bubble" in housing prices is unlikely to occur anytime soon. But a home whose total carrying cost is comfortably within your income—roughly one-quarter of your gross—and is slated to be mortgage-free by retirement age is still a good investment. It's also one of the few tax shelters available to most of the middle class. What's more, through increasingly popular "reverse mortgages," it can become a supplemental source of further retirement income. Like most clichés, this one is still true: "There's no place like home."

NOTES

Note: Unless otherwise noted, the authors have used data from the *1995 Annual Report of the Board of Trustees of the Federal Old-Age and Survivors Insurance and Disability Insurance Trust Fund.*

CHAPTER 1

1. Social Security Administration, *Fast Facts & Figures About Social Security* (Washington, D.C., 1995), 7.
2. *Retirement in the 21st Century: Ready or Not* (Washington, D.C.: Employee Benefit Research Institute, 1994), 7.
3. *Fast Facts & Figures About Social Security,* 5.
4. *Who Will Pay for Your Retirement? The Looming Crisis* (New York: Committee for Economic Development, 1995), 17.
5. Social Security Administration, "1996 Social Security Changes Announced," news release, 13 October 1995, 3.
6. Social Security Administration, *1995 Annual Report of the Board of Trustees of the Federal Old-Age and Survivors Insurance and Disability Insurance Trust Funds* (Washington, D.C., 1995), 122. Hereafter referred to as *1995 Annual Report of the Board of Trustees.*
7. Edward Cowan, "Carter Signs Social Security Tax Rise for 110 Million," *The New York Times,* 21 December 1977, A19.
8. Robert J. Myers, *Social Security,* Fourth Edition (Philadelphia: Pension Research Council and University of Pennsylvania Press, 1993), 893.
9. "Social Security: The Credibility Gap," summary of results of 8–10 September 1994, survey by the Luntz Research Companies in conjunction with Mark A. Siegel Associates for Third Millennium, 1.

CHAPTER 2

1. Spencer Rich, "Baby Boomers' Retirement Could Be a Bust, Living Standards May Drop as Social Security Rolls Bulge," *The Washington Post*, 27 June 1995, A1.

2. U.S. Bureau of the Census, *Historical Statistics of the United States: Colonial Times to 1970, Part I* (Washington, D.C., 1976), 49; and U.S. Bureau of the Census, *Population Projections of the United States by Age, Sex, Race, and Hispanic Origin: 1995 to 2050* (Washington, D.C., 1993), 44.

3. *1995 Annual Report of the Board of Trustees*, 6, 23–30, 183; and Social Security and Medicare Boards of Trustees, *Status of the Social Security and Medicare Programs: A Summary of the 1995 Annual Reports* (Washington, D.C., April 1995), 7–8, 13.

4. *1995 Annual Report of the Board of Trustees*, 122.

5. Social Security Administration, Office of the Actuary, "Illustrative Social Security Retirement Benefit Amounts, and Number of Months To Recover the Value of Past Social Security Taxes, for Beneficiaries Retiring in 1975, 1985, 1995, 2015, and 2035," memorandum, 12 April 1995, 7.

6. Social Security Administration, *Understanding Social Security* (Washington, D.C.: April 1994), 11–12.

7. *1995 Annual Report of the Board of Trustees*, 23–30, 183; and calculations by Bruce D. Schobel based on Social Security benefits and tax data.

8. *1995 Annual Report of the Board of Trustees*, 122.

9. Ibid., 26, 183.

10. *The 1993 Annual Report of the Federal Old-Age and Survivors Insurance and Disability Insurance Trust Fund* (Washington, D.C.: Social Security Board of Trustees, 7 April 1993), 3, 6.

11. *1995 Annual Report of the Board of Trustees*, 122.

12. Ibid., 183; and calculations by Bruce D. Schobel based on Social Security benefits and tax data.

13. Sarah Glazer, "Overhauling Social Security," *CQ Researcher*, vol. 5, no. 18, 12 May 1995, 419.

14. Robert Lukefahr, written statement presented at a hearing of the Advisory Council on Social Security, Washington, D.C., 8 March 1995, 2.

15. *1995 Annual Report of the Board of Trustees*, 66, 177, 185.

16. "Illustrative Social Security Retirement Benefit Amounts, and Number of Months to Recover the Value of Past Social Security Taxes, for Beneficiaries Retiring in 1975, 1985, 1995, 2015, and 2035," 8.

17. Ibid., 1; and *1995 Annual Report of the Board of Trustees*, 56.

18. "Illustrative Social Security Retirement Benefit Amounts, and Number of Months To Recover the Value of Past Social Security Taxes, for Beneficiaries Retiring in 1975, 1985, 1995, 2015, and 2035," 3.

19. Lukefahr, written statement, 2.

20. John C. Rother, "Options for the Future," *Modern Maturity*, July–August 1995, 100.

21. Dorcas R. Hardy and C. Colburn Hardy, *Social Insecurity* (New York: Villard Books, 1991), 27–28.

22. *The Zero Deficit Plan: A Plan for Eliminating the Federal Budget Deficit by the Year 2002* (Washington, D.C.: The Concord Coalition, May 1995), 30.

23. William G. Shipman, "Retiring with Dignity: Social Security vs. Private Markets," SSP No. 2, Cato Institute, 14 August 1995, 4.

24. *Status of the Social Security and Medicare Programs: A Summary of the 1995 Annual Reports,* 11.

25. Sylvester J. Schieber and Laurene A. Graig, *U.S. Retirement Policy: The Sleeping Giant Awakens* (Washington, D.C.: The Wyatt Company, 1994), 21.

26. *Bipartisan Commission on Entitlement and Tax Reform: Final Report to the President* (Washington, D.C.: Government Printing Office, January 1995), 232.

27. *U.S. Retirement Policy: The Sleeping Giant Awakens,* 21.

28. *The Concord Coalition: Citizens for America's Future* (Commerce, California: The Concord Coalition, 1992), 12.

29. *1978 Annual Report of the Board of Trustees of the Federal Old-Age and Survivors Insurance and Disability Insurance Trust Funds* (Washington, D.C.: Social Security Board of Trustees), 2.

30. Francis X. Clines, "Pension Changes Signed into Law," *The New York Times,* 21 April 1983, A17.

31. "Taxes and the American Family," chart, Tax Foundation, Washington, D.C., 1995.

32. Glazer, "Overhauling Social Security," 421.

33. Calculations by Bruce D. Schobel based on Social Security tax and benefit data.

34. Personal interview with Bruce D. Schobel, Princeton, New Jersey, 23 September 1995.

35. *1995 Annual Report of the Board of Trustees,* 61.

36. Ibid., 122.

37. Ibid., 61.

38. *Who Will Pay for Your Retirement? The Looming Crisis,* 26–27.

39. Hardy and Hardy, *Social Insecurity,* 21.

40. Ibid., 18.

41. Social Security Board, *Security in Your Old Age* (Washington, D.C., 1936), 2.

42. Myers, *Social Security,* 13–14.

43. *Security in Your Old Age,* 4.

44. Barney Crosier, "Social Security's First Lady Was a Vermonter," *The Rutland Daily Herald,* 21 August 1985, 4A.

CHAPTER 3

1. *Bartlett's Familiar Quotations,* 16th ed. (Boston: Little, Brown, 1992), 648.

2. "The President's Message," *The New York Times,* 9 June 1934, 1–2.

3. Ibid., 2.

4. Ibid., 2.

5. K. B. Smeillie, *Great Britain Since 1688: A Modern History* (Ann Arbor: The University of Michigan Press, 1962), 400.

6. Arthur J. Schlesinger, Jr., *The Coming of the New Deal* (Boston: Houghton Mifflin, 1959), 312.

7. Arthur J. Altmeyer, *The Formative Years of Social Security* (Madison: The University of Wisconsin Press, 1968), 9–11.

8. William Ivy Hair, *The Kingfish and His Realm: The Life and Times of Huey P. Long* (Baton Rouge: Louisiana State University Press, 1991), 269–270.

9. Social Security Administration, *A Brief History of the Social Security Administration* (Washington, D.C., March 1995), 4.

10. Myers, *Social Security,* 15.

11. *Security in Your Old Age,* 1, 2, 4.

12. Data gathered in interview with staff member, Historian's Office, Social Security Administration, 10 July 1995.

13. Robert M. Ball, "The 1939 Amendments to the Social Security Act and What Followed," Chapter 6, 50th Anniversary Edition, *The Report of the Committee on Economic Security of 1935* (Washington, D.C.: National Conference on Social Welfare, 1985), 163–167.

CHAPTER 4

1. Altmeyer, *The Formative Years of Social Security,* 3.

2. Fritz Stern, *Gold and Iron: Bismarck, Bleichroder, and the Building of the German Empire* (New York: Alfred A. Knopf, 1977), 219.

3. John C. Goodman, *Social Security in the United Kingdom: Contracting Out of the System* (Washington, D.C.: American Enterprise Institute for Public Policy Research), 7.

4. Roy Lubove, *The Struggle for Social Security 1900–1935,* Second Edition (Pittsburgh: University of Pittsburgh Press, 1986), 119.

5. Ibid., 120–122.

6. Ibid., 123–124.

7. Theodore Zeldin, *France 1848–1945,* Volume One (Oxford: Oxford University Press, 1973), 409, 487, 660, 663.

8. Ibid., 660.

9. Carolyn L. Weaver, *The Crisis in Social Security: Economic and Political Origins* (Durham: Duke Press Policy Studies, 1982), 33.

10. Edward Cranksaw, *Bismarck* (New York: The Viking Press, 1981), 45, 290–292, 360, 378.

11. Franklin D. Scott, *Scandinavia* (Cambridge: Harvard University Press, 1975), 76–77.

12. Weaver, *The Crisis in Social Security,* 33–35.

13. T. O. Lloyd, *Empire to Welfare State: English History 1906–1985,* Third Edition (Oxford: Oxford University Press, 1986), 14.
14. Ted Morgan, *Churchill: Young Man in a Hurry, 1874–1915* (New York: Simon and Schuster, 1982), 229–230.
15. Weaver, *The Crisis in Social Security,* 33–34.
16. Social Security Administration, *Social Security Programs Throughout the World—1995* (Washington, D.C., 1995), p. xlii.
17. *Averting the Old Age Crisis: Policies to Protect the Old and Promote Growth,* A World Bank Policy Research Report (New York: Oxford University Press, 1994), 26–27, 30.
18. Ibid., 25, 73, 280–281.
19. Ibid., xiii.
20. Congressional Research Service, "Privatizing Social Security as Chile Did," memorandum (Washington, D.C., February 10, 1995), 2.
21. *Averting the Old Age Crisis,* xiii.

CHAPTER 5

1. National Resources Planning Board, Warren S. Thompson and P. K. Whelpton, *Estimates of Future Population of the United States 1940–2000* (Washington, D.C., 1943), 29, 43.
2. *Historical Statistics of the United States: Colonial Times to 1970,* 49.
3. William Dunn, "Middle-Aged Baby Boomers Will Set the Pace," *USA Today,* 14 September 1987, 6E.
4. U.S. Bureau of the Census, *Population Projections of the United States by Age, Sex, Race, and Hispanic Origin: 1995 to 2050* (Washington, D.C., 1996), 44.
5. *1995 World Population Data Sheet* (Washington, D.C.: Population Reference Bureau, 1995), 1–4.
6. William Dunn, "Oldies Rock Around Dial," *USA Today,* 26 July 1990, 1A.
7. Altmeyer, *The Formative Years of Social Security,* 185.
8. *1995 Annual Report of the Board of Trustees,* 35.
9. Robert F. Burk, *Dwight D. Eisenhower: Hero and Politician* (Boston: Twayne Publishers, 1986), 114.
10. Ibid., 154.
11. Stephen E. Ambrose, *Eisenhower: Soldier, General of the Army, President-Elect, 1890–1952,* Volume One (New York: Simon and Schuster, 1983), 568.
12. *1995 Annual Report of the Board of Trustees,* 35, 122.
13. Altmeyer, *The Formative Years of Social Security,* 286.
14. *A Brief History of the Social Security Administration,* 12.
15. *1995 Annual Report of the Board of Trustees,* 170.
16. James M. Naughton, "McGovern Attacks Nixon as Boston Crowd Cheers," *The New York Times,* 4 October 1972, 32.
17. *1995 Annual Report of the Board of Trustees,* 35, 122, 170.

18. Martha Derthick, *Policymaking for Social Security* (Washington, D.C.: The Brookings Institution, 1979), 166.
19. *Statistical Abstract of the United States 1993,* 399.
20. U.S. Bureau of the Census, Current Population Survey, unpublished data.
21. *Statistical Abstract of the United States 1994,* 386.
22. *1995 Annual Report of the Board of Trustees,* 122.
23. Ibid., 122.

CHAPTER 6

1. Arthur B. Kennickell and Martha Starr-McCluer, "Changes in Family Finances from 1989 to 1992: Evidence from the Survey of Consumer Finances," *Federal Reserve Bulletin,* October 1994, 863–864.
2. Ibid., 864–866.
3. Ibid., 869.
4. Ibid., 865.
5. "Third Annual Merrill Lynch Study Finds Baby Boom Retirement Savings Rate Putting a Generation in Crisis," news release, Merrill Lynch & Co., 17 April 1995, 2.
6. B. Douglas Bernheim, *The Merrill Lynch Baby Boom Retirement Index: Update '95* (sponsored by Merrill Lynch & Co., February 1995), 19–20.
7. "Third Annual Merrill Lynch Study Finds Baby Boom Retirement Savings Rate Putting a Generation in Crisis," 5.
8. "Execs Need Retirement Savings, Too," *Business Insurance,* 29 May 1995, 34.
9. *Statistical Abstract of the United States 1994,* 863.
10. U.S. Department of Commerce, Bureau of Economic Analysis, unpublished chart based on *National Income and Product Accounts,* annual reports 1929–1994 (Washington, D.C.), 1–2.
11. Ibid., 1.
12. Ibid., 1–2.
13. Ibid., 2.
14. Janet L. Fix and Phillip Fiorini, "Supersavers Get Jump on Golden Years," *USA Today,* 24 May 1995, 1A–2A.
15. Bernard Wysocki, Jr., "Binge Buyers: Many Baby Boomers Save Little, May Run into Trouble Later On . . . ," *The Wall Street Journal,* 5 June 1995, A1.
16. Fix and Fiorini, "Supersavers Get Jump on Golden Years," 1A.
17. *1995 Annual Report of the Board of Trustees,* 35, 170.
18. *Understanding Social Security,* 31.
19. "Taxes and the American Family," chart, Tax Foundation (Washington, D.C., 1995).
20. W. Thomas Kelly, *Wealth Is Not a Dirty Word* (Paoli, Pennsylvania: Mill Run Press, 1994), 4.
21. Ibid., 4.
22. *Fast Facts & Figures About Social Security,* 7.

23. U.S. Department of Labor, *Private Pension Plan Bulletin,* Number 4 (Washington, D.C., Winter 1995), 63.
24. Alicia H. Munnell, "Current Taxation of Qualified Pension Plans: Has the Time Come?" *New England Economic Review,* March/April 1992, 24.
25. Everett T. Allen, Jr., Joseph J. Melone, Jerry S. Rosenbloom, and Jack L. VanDerhet, *Pension Planning: Pensions, Profit-Sharing, and Other Deferred Compensation Plans,* Sixth Edition (Homewood, Illinois: Irwin, 1998), 1–2.
26. Marshall N. Carter, "Trends in World Financial Markets," speech, Boston Economic Club, 5 April 1995, 9.
27. Lane Kirkland, "Be Wary of Trend to 401(K) Plans," *USA Today,* 10 May 1995, 13A.
28. Carter, "Trends in World Financial Markets," 11.
29. Sylvester J. Schieber and Laurene A. Graig, *U.S. Retirement Policy: The Sleeping Giant Awakens* (Washington, D.C., The Wyatt Company, 1994), 8.
30. Ibid., 36–37.
31. Carter, "Trends in World Financial Markets," 10.

CHAPTER 7

1. *Historical Statistics of the United States: Colonial Times to 1970,* Part I, 49, and *Statistical Abstract of the United States 1994,* 75.
2. *Population Projections of the United States, by Age, Sex, Race, and Hispanic Origin: 1995 to 2050,* 44.
3. Heather Lamm, member of the board of directors of Third Millennium, prepared statement presented to the Senate Subcommittee on Social Security and Family Policy, 27 June 1995, 2, 5.
4. Third Millennium, 18–34 Survey, The Luntz Companies/Mark A. Siegel and Associates, Interview Schedule, 3.
5. Glazer, "Overhauling Social Security," 434.
6. Social Security benefit calculation by Bruce Schobel is based on 1995 Social Security benefits and tax data, and assumes that the worker paid OASDI payroll taxes on average wages beginning at age twenty-one and continuing until retirement at age sixty-seven. It is further assumed that Social Security continues operating under present law.
7. "Illustrative Social Security Retirement Benefit Amounts, and Number of Months to Recover the Value of Past Social Security Taxes, for Beneficiaries Retiring in 1975, 1985, 1995, 2015, and 2035," 8.
8. *1995 Annual Report of the Board of Trustees,* 122.
9. *Bipartisan Commission on Entitlement and Tax Reform: Final Report to the President,* 25.
10. "20-Somethings No Slackers When It Comes to Retirement Planning, According to Kemper-Roper Retirement Monitor," news release on poll findings, Kemper Financial Services, 15 June 1995, 2.

11. Ibid., 2.

12. Ibid., 1.

13. *Statistical Abstract of the United States 1994,* 76.

14. Suzanne M. Bianchi, *America's Children: Mixed Prospects,* (Washington, D.C.: Population Reference Bureau, June 1990), 17.

15. Ibid., 9–10.

16. Eric L. Dey, Alexander W. Astin, William S. Korn, and Ellyne R. Riggs, *The American Freshman: National Norms for Fall 1992* (Los Angeles: Higher Education Research Institute, University of California, Los Angeles, 1992), 4.

17. Dunn, *The Baby Bust: A Generation Comes of Age,* 64–65.

18. *Digest of Education Statistics 1992,* 17, 184.

19. Roger D. Semerad, U.S. Department of Labor, undated press release summarizing results of *Work Force 2000* (Washington, D.C., 1987), 4.

20. *Statistical Abstract of the United States 1994,* 412.

21. Glazer, "Overhauling Social Security," 426.

22. Randall Lane, "Computers Are Our Friends," *Forbes,* 8 May 1995, 102.

23. Alan Deutschman, "What 25-Year-Olds Want," *Fortune,* 27 August 1990, 43.

24. Ibid.

25. Neil Howe and William Strauss, "The New Generation Gap," *The Atlantic,* December 1992, 68.

26. Martha Farnsworth Riche, "The Boomerang Age," *American Demographics,* May 1990, 25.

27. "Generating Change," *The Next Progressive,* January 1993, 5.

CHAPTER 8

1. Cowan, "Carter Signs Social Security Tax Rise for 110 Million," A19.

2. Ibid.

3. *1995 Annual Report of the Board of Trustees,* 35.

4. Myers, *Social Security,* 893.

5. Ibid., 893–894.

6. Francis X. Clines, "Pension Changes Signed Into Law," *The New York Times,* 21 April 1983, A17.

7. Myers, *Social Security,* 101–102.

8. U.S. Bureau of the Census, *Income, Poverty, and Valuation of Noncash Benefits: 1993* (Washington, D.C., 1993), XV; and *Chronicle of the World* (London: ECAM Publications, 1989), 1142.

9. *Statistical Abstract of the United States 1994,* 395, 488.

10. *Bipartisan Commission on Entitlement and Tax Reform: Final Report to the President,* 27.

11. David Shribman, "The Social Security Crisis: Legacy of Hopeful Guesses," *The New York Times,* 5 January 1983, A1, D20.

12. Ibid., D20.

13. *Statistical Abstract of the United States 1994,* 8.

14. *Bipartisan Commission on Entitlement and Tax Reform: Final Report to the President*, 27.

15. Edward Cowan, "Carter Asks Rise in Taxes to Aid Social Security," *The New York Times*, 8 May 1977, 1.

16. Ronald Reagan, *An American Life: Ronald Reagan/The Autobiography* (New York: Simon and Schuster, 1990), 313.

17. David A. Stockman, *The Triumph of Politics: How the Reagan Revolution Failed* (New York: Harper & Row, 1986), 190–191.

18. Ibid., 13.

19. Steven Mufson and Dana Priest, "Clinton Signals Intention to Confront the Federal Budget Deficit," *Washington Post*, 19 December 1992, A9.

20. Bob Woodward, *The Agenda: Inside the Clinton White House* (New York: Simon & Schuster, 1994), 106.

21. Ibid.

22. Gwen Ifill, "Social Security Won't Be Subject to a Benefit Freeze, Clinton Says," *The New York Times*, 9 February 1993, A1.

23. President Bill Clinton, "The State of the Union," *Washington Post*, 18 February 1993, A25.

24. Ruth Marcus and Ann Devroy, "Asking Americans to 'Face Facts,' Clinton Presents Plan to Raise Taxes, Cut Deficit," *Washington Post*, 18 February 1993, A22.

25. *Understanding Social Security*, 31.

26. Statement of U.S. Senator Judd Gregg, *Bipartisan Commission on Entitlement and Tax Reform: Final Report to the President*, unnumbered attachment.

27. Robert Pear, "Plan to Put Part of Social Security into Stock Funds," *The New York Times*, 17 February 1996, 1.

28. Ibid., 10.

29. Mike McNamee, "Privatize Social Security? Nobody's Laughing Now," *Business Week*, 5 February 1996, 55.

30. William M. Welch, "Social Security Is Pushed Back onto Table for Debate," *USA Today*, 18 May 1995, 12A.

31. "The Kerrey–Simpson Proposal," summary, Office of Senator Bob Kerrey, Washington, D.C., 9.

32. Ibid., 7.

33. Ibid., 5–8.

34. Christopher Georges, "Forbes's Proposal to Restructure Social Security Suggests System Is No Longer Political Third Rail," *The Wall Street Journal*, 9 February 1996, A16.

35. Ibid.

36. *Who Will Pay for Your Retirement? The Looming Crisis*, 2, 6, 8, 14.

37. Lukefahr, prepared statement presented at a hearing of the Advisory Council on Social Security, 2.

38. Ibid., 2–3.

39. "Social Security: The Credibility Gap," summary of results of the 1994 Third Millennium Survey, 1–6.

40. Lukefahr, prepared statement presented at a hearing of the Advisory Council on Social Security, 2.
41. Allan Tull, prepared statement by the American Association of Retired Persons, presented at a hearing to the Senate Finance Committee, Subcommittee on Social Security and Family Policy, 27 June 1995, 1, 3.

CHAPTER 9

1. Social Security Administration, *Social Security Bulletin: Annual Statistical Supplement* (Washington, D.C., 1994), 247.
2. William G. Poortvliet and Thomas P. Laine, "A Global Trend: Privatization and Reform of Social Security Pension Plans," *Benefits Quarterly,* Third Quarter 1995, 72.
3. "A Mountain of Money," *The Economist,* 22 April 1995, 17.
4. Jose Pinera, "Chileans Unravel Social-Security Tangle," *The Wall Street Journal,* 3 January 1986, 13.
5. G. Ricardo Campbell, "Chile and Mexico Privatize Social Security," *Journal of International Compensation & Benefits,* July/August 1993, 7–8.
6. Julio Bustmente Geraldo, *Social Security Reform in Chile* (Association of Pension Fund Administrators), 1–9.
7. Campbell, "Chile and Mexico Privatize Social Security," 8.
8. Pinera, "Chileans Unravel Social-Security Tangle," 13.
9. Geraldo, *Social Security Reform in Chile,* 4–9.
10. *The Chilean Private Pension System* (Santiago: The International Center for Pension Reform, 1995), 7–8.
11. Margaret Price, "Chile Relaxes Rules for Domestic Funds," *Pensions & Investments,* 12 June 1995, 12.
12. *The Chilean Private Pension System,* 5–7.
13. Ibid., 8.
14. U.S. Bureau of the Census, *Statistical Abstract of the United States 1995* (Washington, D.C., 1995), 848.
15. Patricia Harteneck and Douglas J. Carey, "The New Direction in South American Pension Plans," *Journal of International Compensation & Benefits,* March/April 1994, 28.
16. Campbell, "Chile and Mexico Privatize Social Security," 12.
17. G. Ricardo Campbell, "Privatization in Peru, Italy, and Argentina," *Journal of International Compensation & Benefits,* January/February 1994, 31.
18. Maria Kielmas, "Italy Passes Pension Reforms," *Business Insurance,* 24 July 1995, 17.
19. *Social Security Programs Throughout the World—1995,* 177.
20. Kielmas, "Italy Passes Pension Reforms," 17.
21. Goodman, *Social Security in the United Kingdom: Contracting Out of the System,* 1.

22. Ibid., 55.

23. "The Welfare State; Time for Reform," *The Economist*, 10 June 1995.

24. Margaret Thatcher, *The Downing Street Years* (New York: Harper-Collins, 1993), 677.

25. Hugo Young, *The Iron Lady* (New York: Farrar Straus Giroux, 1989), 47.

26. Thatcher, *The Downing Street Years*, 673.

27. "The State and Occupational Pension Systems: Summary" (United Kingdom Department of Social Security), 2.

28. *Averting the Old Age Crisis*, 201.

29. *Social Security Programs Throughout the World—1995*, 15.

30. Margaret Price, "Australia's Pension Maze: Complex System Shifts Burden Away from Government," *Pensions & Investments*, 18 April 1994, 21.

31. Australian Department of the Treasury, "1995 Budget: Budget Boosts National Savings Via Superannuation," press release, 1.

32. Price, "Australia's Pension Maze," 21.

33. "1995 Budget: Budget Boosts National Savings Via Superannuation," 1.

34. Ibid.

35. Social Security Administration, *Social Security Programs Throughout the World—1993* (Washington, D.C., 1994), 310.

36. K. G. Scherman, "The Swedish Experience," report to a roundtable discussion during the 7th Annual Conference of the National Academy of Social Insurance (Washington, D.C., 26 January 1995), 30.

37. *Social Security Programs Throughout the World—1995*, 316.

38. Scherman, "The Swedish Experience," 12.

39. The National Board of Health and Welfare, *Growing Old in Sweden* (Stockholm, 1993), 48.

CHAPTER 10

1. The PSSA assumes a 5.3 percent payroll contribution based on average wages beginning this year and ending with the year preceding retirement. The PSSA earns a preretirement return of 10 percent annually. The accumulated fund buys an annuity to age eighty (approximate life expectancy), which earns a postretirement return of 7 percent annually. The annuity benefit increases 4 percent annually, the assumed inflation rate. This and all other PSSA calculations in Part II were done by Bruce D. Schobel, an actuary at the Social Security Administration from 1979 to 1988.

2. This and all subsequent Social Security benefit calculations by Bruce Schobel are based on 1995 Social Security data, computed under present law, using average earnings starting with age twenty-one. It is further assumed that Social Security continues to operate under present law. Social Security's normal age of retirement figures are used, which are explained in the Social Security Administration booklet *Understanding Social Security*, 14.

3. Shipman, "Retiring with Dignity: Social Security vs. Private Markets" (Chicago: Ibbotson Associates, 1996), 6. Values are derived from *Stocks, Bonds, Bills and Inflation* (Chicago: Ibbotson Associates, 1995).

4. Shipman, "Retiring with Dignity: Social Security vs. Private Markets," 6.

CHAPTER 11

1. Ellen E. Schultz, "Frittered Away: Offered a Lump Sum, Many Retirees Blow It and Risk Their Future," *Wall Street Journal*, 31 July 1995, A1.

2. Ibid.

3. Ibid.

4. *Statistical Abstract of the United States 1995*, 86.

5. *1995 Annual Report of the Board of Trustees*, 62.

6. The PSSA calculation by Bruce Schobel assumes payroll contributions based on average wages beginning this year and ending with the year preceding retirement. The PSSA earns a preretirement return of 10 percent annually. The accumulated fund buys an annuity to age eighty (approximate life expectancy) that earns a postretirement return of 7 percent annually. The annuity benefit increases 4 percent annually, the assumed inflation rate.

7. The Social Security calculations by Bruce Schobel are based on 1995 Social Security data, computed under present law, using average wages.

8. Social Security Administration, "1996 Social Security Changes Announced," news release, 13 October 1995, 1, 3.

9. *Understanding Social Security*, 14.

10. *1995 Annual Report of the Board of Trustees*, 122.

CHAPTER 12

1. PSSA calculations are by Bruce Schobel. The Social Security calculations, also by Schobel, are based on 1995 Social Security benefits and tax data, computed under present law, using average wages starting at age twenty-one.

2. Shipman, "Retiring with Dignity: Social Security vs. Private Markets," values derived from *Stocks, Bonds, Bills and Inflation*, 6.

3. *1995 Annual Report of the Board of Trustees*, 62.

CHAPTER 13

1. Social Security's retirement liability, computed by Bruce Schobel, is based on 1995 Social Security benefits and payroll tax data, as well as Social Security's worker/beneficiary projections, and assumes that Social Security continues operating under present law.

2. The present value deficit calculation (1995–2069) by Bruce Schobel uses 1995 Social Security benefits and payroll tax data, as well as worker/

beneficiary projections, and assumes the continuation of Social Security under present law.

3. Telephone interview with Bruce Schobel, 18 March 1996.

4. Calculations by Bruce Schobel assume that all eligible workers will join a PSSA plan in 1996 and begin contributing to their PSSAs, with PSSAs earning a preretirement annual return of 10 percent. Those same workers will have stopped their OASDI payroll tax contributions to Social Security in 1995. Employers, however, would continue to pay payroll tax to Social Security under present law.

5. Ibid.

6. Ibid.

7. Ibid.

CHAPTER 14

1. Social Security Administration, "1996 Social Security Changes," fact sheet (Washington, D.C., 13 October 1995), 1.

2. *1995 Annual Report of the Board of Trustees,* 36.

3. PSSA calculations by Bruce Schobel assume 7 percent contributions beginning this year and ending in the year preceding retirement, with the PSSA fund earning an annual preretirement return of 10 percent. Wage earnings are assumed to be the national average for this and all subsequent work years. The PSSA will fund an annuity to age eighty, the approximate life expectancy. The postretirement return on the annuity funds will be 7 percent. Annuity benefits will increase 4 percent annually, the assumed rate of inflation. Social Security's replacement rate is explained on pages 11–12 of its publication *Understanding Social Security.* The normal age of retirement is explained in the same publication on page 14.

4. *A Brief History of the Social Security Administration,* 4.

5. The PSSA assumptions are the same as those detailed in endnote 3 of this chapter.

6. Ibid.

7. Ibid.

8. Ibid.

9. Ibid.

10. Ibid.

11. Ibid.

12. Ibid.

13. Deficit calculations by Bruce Schobel are based on Social Security benefits, payroll tax data, and worker/beneficiary projections, and assume that the system continues under present law. It is further assumed that everyone eligible to join a PSSA does join and makes contributions based on average wages, while ending their OASDI payroll tax contributions to Social Security in 1995. It is also assumed that all employers continue to pay OASDI payroll taxes to Social Security.

14. Ibid.
15. Ibid.
16. Surplus calculations by Bruce Schobel assume all eligible workers join a PSSA and contribute 7 percent of their average earnings beginning in 1996. The same workers end their OASDI payroll tax contributions to Social Security in 1995. It is further assumed that Social Security continues to operate under present law, with employers paying 5.3 percent OASDI taxes.
17. Social Security annual deficit calculations by Bruce Schobel are based on Social Security benefits and payroll tax data, as well as worker/employer projections, and assume that the system continues operating under present law.
18. *Fast Facts & Figures about Social Security,* 7.

CHAPTER 15

1. John Meehan and Jeffrey M. Laderman, "The Smart 401(k)," *Business Week,* 3 July 1995, 61.
2. Ibid.
3. Ibid., 58.
4. Ibid.
5. *Saving the American Dream: An Economic and Public Opinion Study* (Merrill Lynch & Co., April 1994), 18.
6. "Help America To Save," *Retirement Advisor* (Merrill Lynch & Co., June 1995), 4.
7. Hardy and Hardy, *Social Insecurity,* 58.
8. Craig S. Karpel, *The Retirement Myth* (New York: HarperCollins, 1995), 35.
9. Bipartisan Commission on Entitlement and Tax Reform, *Bipartisan Commission on Entitlement and Tax Reform: Interim Report to the President* (Washington, D.C., August 1994), 5.
10. U.S. Department of the Treasury, *Monthly of the Public Debt of the United States* (Washington, D.C.), Table 1.
11. Social Security liability calculations by Bruce Schobel are based on 1995 Social Security benefits and payroll tax data, as well as worker/beneficiary projections, and assume that Social Security continues to operate under present law.
12. *Saving the American Dream,* 4.
13. *Retirement in the 21st Century: Ready or Not,* 39–40.
14. Paul S. Hewitt, "The Problem with Social Security," introduction, *Entitlements and the Aging of America,* 1994 NTUF Chartbook (Washington, D.C.: National Taxpayer's Union Foundation, 1994), 8.
15. Jeffrey M. Laderman and Russell Mitchell, "A Capital Gains Cut Won't Gore Wall Street," *Business Week,* 10 July 1995, 116.

16. Connie Mack, "Capital Gains Taxes—A $1.5 Trillion Opportunity," *The Wall Street Journal,* 29 August 1995, A14.
17. Carter, "Trends in World Financial Markets," 10.
18. Ibid., 9.
19. *Saving the American Dream,* 17.
20. Carter, "Trends in World Financial Markets," 11.
21. John A. Turner, *Pension Policy for a Mobile Labor Force* (Kalamazoo: W. E. Upjohn Institute, 1993), 52–53.
22. *Baby Boomers in Retirement: An Early Perspective,* 44.
23. Robert B. Avery and Michael S. Rendall, "Estimating the Size and Distribution of Baby Boomers' Prospective Inheritances," findings presented at the annual meeting of the American Statistical Association (Alexandria, Virginia, 1993), 3.
24. *Baby Boomers in Retirement: An Early Perspective,* 29.
25. *Retirement in the 21st Century: Ready or Not,* 15.
26. Ibid., 3.
27. *Statistical Abstract of the United States 1995,* 736.
28. *The State of the Nation's Housing 1992* (Cambridge, Massachusetts: Joint Center for Housing Studies of Harvard University, 1992), 12.
29. *The State of the Nation's Housing 1995* (Cambridge, Massachusetts: Joint Center for Housing Studies of Harvard University, 1995), 5.
30. Ibid.

CHAPTER 16

1. *Retirement in the 21st Century: Ready or Not,* 7.
2. *Fast Facts & Figures About Social Security,* 6.
3. Ibid., 5.
4. *Who Will Pay for Your Retirement? The Looming Crisis,* 17.
5. *Fast Facts & Figures About Social Security,* 6.
6. Hewitt, introduction, *Entitlements and the Aging of America,* 6.
7. Ibid.
8. PSSA and Social Security calculations by Bruce Schobel assume a PSSA worker contribution of 7 percent and a PSSA employer contribution of 6 percent on average wages beginning this year, compared to Social Security under present law.
9. U.S. Department of Labor, *Consumer Expenditures in 1993* (Washington, D.C., 1994), 3–4.
10. Social Security Administration, Table 2, "Amount of OASDI benefits in current-payment status, by type of benefit, by sex of beneficiaries aged 65 or older, and by State, December 1993," 2.
11. William Dunn, "Seniors Pose a Challenge for Towns," *USA Today,* 5–7 April 1991, 1A–2A.
12. William Dunn, "From Dust Bowl to Desirable," *USA Today,* 18–20 August 1989, 3A.

CHAPTER 17

1. "A new face. A new voice. A new market," advertisement for *Modern Maturity,* appearing in *The New York Times,* 18 September 1995, D9.
2. Executive Committee policy statement, PAC 20/20, 9 January 1995, 1.
3. Robert J. Myers, *Expansionism in Social Insurance* (Westminster, England: The Institute of Economic Affairs, 1970), 15, 29.
4. Derthick, *Policymaking for Social Security,* 188–189.

INDEX